Essential Arabic

Edited by

Christopher Warnasch and Rana K. Casteel

Content in this program has been modified and enhanced from *Starting Out in Arabic*, published in 2008.

Living Language is a member of the Random House Information Group

Published in the United States by Living Language, an imprint of Random House, Inc.

www.livinglanguage.com

Editor: Christopher Warnasch
Production Editor: Ciara Robinson
Production Manager: Tom Marshall
Interior Design: Sophie Chin
Illustrations: Sophie Chin
Typesetting: worldaccent.com

First Edition

ISBN: 978-0-307-97235-4

Library of Congress Cataloging-in-Publication Data is available upon request.
This book is available at special discounts for bulk purchases for sales promotions or premiums. Special editions, including personalized covers, excerpts of existing books, and corporate imprints, can be created in large quantities for special needs. For more information, write to Special Markets/Premium Sales, 1745 Broadway, MD 3-1, New York, New York 10019 or e-mail specialmarkets@randomhouse.com.

PRINTED IN THE UNITED STATES OF AMERICA

10

Acknowledgments

Thanks to the Living Language team: Amanda D'Acierno, Christopher Warnasch, Suzanne McQuade, Laura Riggio, Erin Quirk, Amanda Munoz, Fabrizio LaRocca, Siobhan O'Hare, Sophie Chin, Sue Daulton, Alison Skrabek, Carolyn Roth, Ciara Robinson, and Tom Marshall.

Audio produced by Ok Hee Kolwitz.

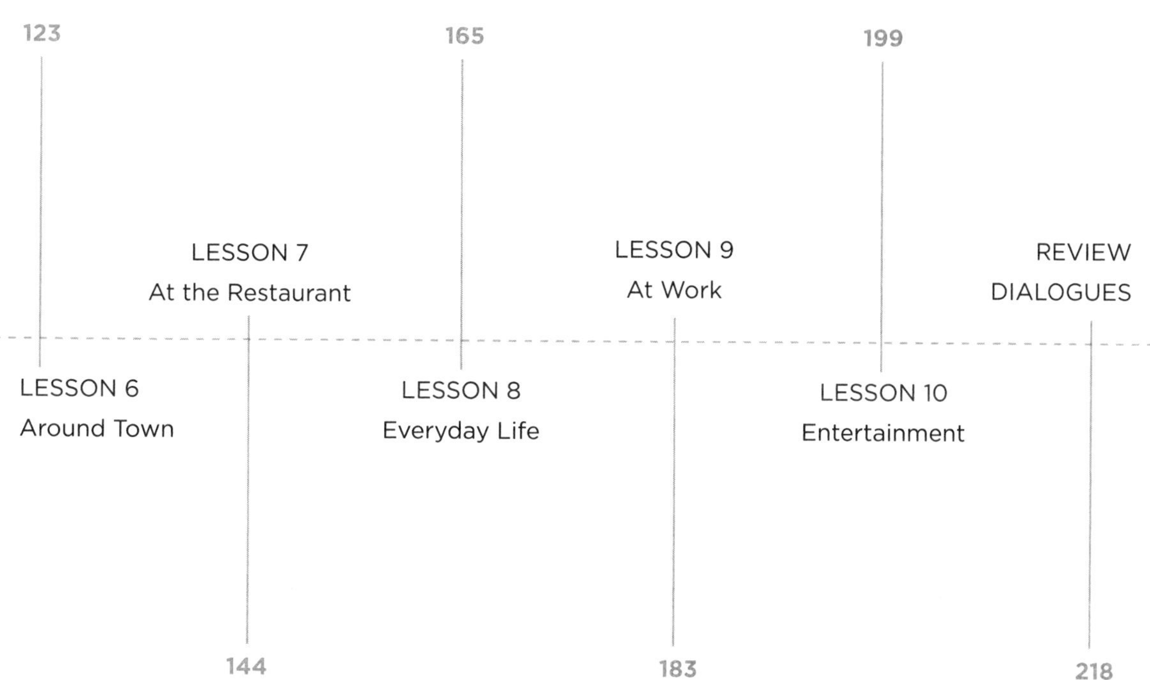

123
LESSON 6
Around Town
144
LESSON 7
At the Restaurant
165
LESSON 8
Everyday Life
183
LESSON 9
At Work
199
LESSON 10
Entertainment
218
REVIEW
DIALOGUES

How to Use This Course

مَرْحَباً **marHaban!**

Welcome to *Living Language Essential Arabic*! Ready to learn how to speak, read, and write Arabic?

Before we begin, let's go over what you'll see in this course. It's very easy to use, but this section will help you get started.

PHONETICS

This course includes both Arabic script and phonetic transcription (in other words, **marHaban** in addition to مَرْحَباً) to help you get started with reading and pronouncing Arabic. However, please keep in mind that phonetics are not exact—they are just an approximation of Arabic sounds using English(-like) spelling—so you should rely mostly on the audio, *not* the phonetics, to improve your pronunciation skills.

For a guide to our phonetics system, see the Pronunciation and Transcription section at the end of the course. To master reading and writing Arabic, use the Guide to Arabic Script included in the *Living Language Essential Arabic*, *Living Language Complete Arabic*, and *Living Language Platinum Arabic* packages.

LESSONS

There are 10 lessons in this course. Each lesson is divided into three parts and has the following components:

Welcome at the beginning outlining what you will cover in each of the three parts of the lesson.

PART 1

- **Vocabulary Builder 1** listing the key words and phrases for that lesson.
- **Vocabulary Practice 1** to practice what you learned in Vocabulary Builder 1.
- **Grammar Builder 1** to guide you through the structure of the Arabic language (how to form sentences, questions, and so on).

PART 2

- **Vocabulary Builder 2** listing more key words and phrases.
- **Vocabulary Practice 2** to practice what you learned in Vocabulary Builder 2.
- **Grammar Builder 2** for more information on language structure.
- Work Out 1 for a comprehensive practice of what you've learned so far.

PART 3

- **Bring It All Together** to put what you've learned in a conversational context through a dialogue, monologue, description, or other similar text.
- **Work Out 2** for another helpful practice exercise.

- **Drive It Home** to ingrain an important point of Arabic structure for the long term.

- **Parting Words** outlining what you learned in the lesson.

TAKE IT FURTHER

- **Take It Further** sections are scattered throughout the lesson to provide extra information about the new vocabulary you've just seen, expand on some grammar points, or introduce additional words and phrases. They also point to specific sections of the Guide to Arabic Script, so that you can learn to read and write gradually.

WORD RECALL

- **Word Recall** sections appear in between lessons. They review important vocabulary and grammar from previous lessons, including the one you just finished. These sections will reinforce what you've learned so far in the course, and help you retain the information for the long term.

QUIZZES

This course contains two quizzes: **Quiz 1** is halfway through the course (after Lesson 5), and **Quiz 2** appears after the last lesson (Lesson 10). The quizzes are self-graded so it's easy for you to test your progress and see if you should go back and review.

REVIEW DIALOGUES

There are five **Review Dialogues** at the end of the course, after Quiz 2. These everyday dialogues review what you learned in Lessons 1-10, introduce some new vocabulary and structures, and allow you to become more familiar with conversational Arabic. Each dialogue is followed by comprehension questions that serve as the course's final review.

PROGRESS BAR

You will see a **Progress Bar** on almost every page that has course material. It indicates your current position in the course and lets you know how much progress you're making. Each line in the bar represents a lesson, with the final line representing the Review Dialogues.

AUDIO

Look for this symbol ▶ to help guide you through the audio as you're reading the book. It will tell you which track to listen to for each section that has audio. When you see the symbol, select the indicated track and start listening! If you don't see the symbol, then there isn't any audio for that section.

The audio can be used on its own—in other words, without the book—when you're on the go. Whether in your car or at the gym, you can listen to the audio to brush up on your pronunciation or review what you've learned in the book.

PRONUNCIATION GUIDE, GRAMMAR SUMMARY

At the back of this book you will find a **Pronunciation and Transcription Guide**, and a **Grammar Summary**. The Pronunciation and Transcription Guide provides information on Arabic pronunciation and the phonetic transcription system used in this course. The Grammar Summary contains a helpful, brief overview of key points in the Arabic grammar system.

FREE ONLINE TOOLS

Go to **www.livinglanguage.com/languagelab** to access your free online tools. The tools are organized around the lessons in this course, with audiovisual flashcards and interactive games and quizzes for each lesson. These tools will help you review the vocabulary and grammar that you've seen in the lessons, as well as provide some extra practice with words and phrases related to the lesson's topic.

Lesson 1: Essential Expressions

الدَرْس الأوَّل: تَعبيرات أساسيّة

ad-dars al-'awwal: taxbiraat 'asaasiyya

مَرْحَباً **marHaban!** *Welcome!* In this first lesson of your Arabic course, you'll learn some basic courtesy expressions, greetings, and other useful words and phrases that will get you started speaking Arabic:

- ☐ Greet someone and ask how they're doing
- ☐ Be polite with helpful words like *please* and *thanks*
- ☐ Introduce yourself and meet other people
- ☐ Say other polite phrases like *Excuse me* and *I'm sorry*
- ☐ Use what you've learned in a short, practical conversation between two people meeting for the first time.

First, let's get started with some vocabulary. You'll hear the words and phrases in English first and then in Arabic. Repeat each new word or phrase in the pauses provided every time you hear it. You'll see the English, followed by the Arabic in transcription, and then the Arabic in Arabic script. Don't worry about the script yet; we'll come back to that shortly and explain how to slowly integrate Arabic script into your lessons. Ready?

Look for this symbol to help guide you through the audio as you're reading the book. It will tell you which track to listen to for each section that has audio.

Whenever you see the symbol, select the indicated track and start listening. If you don't see the symbol, then there isn't any audio for that section. Keep in mind that the audio can also be used on its own when you're on the go!

Vocabulary Builder 1

Track: Lesson 1 Vocabulary Builder 1 (Track 1) CD: 1

Yes	نَعَم	**naxam**
No	كَلاّ، لا	**kallaa, laa**
Hello.	أهْلاً.	**'ahlan.**
Good morning.	صَباح الخَيْر.	**SabaaH al-khayr.**
Good afternoon/evening.	مَساء الخَيْر.	**masaa' al-khayr.**
Please.	مِن فَضْلَك.	**min faDlak.**
Of course.	طَبْعاً.	**Tabxan.**
Good-bye.	مَعَ السَلامَة.	**maxa s-salaama.**

Vocabulary Practice 1

Now let's practice what you've learned. Match the English on the left with the Arabic equivalent on the right.

1. *yes* — a. صَباح الخَيْر **SabaaH al-khayr.**
2. *no* — b. مِن فَضْلَك **min faDlak.**
3. *Good evening.* — c. نَعَم **naxam**

4. *Good morning.*
5. *Hello.*
6. *Of course.*
7. *Please.*
8. *Good-bye.*

d. مَع السَلامَة maxa s-salaama.
e. مَساء الخَيْر masaa' al-khayr.
f. لا laa
g. طَبْعاً Tabxan.
h. أهْلاً 'ahlan.

ANSWER KEY

1. c; 2. f; 3. e; 4. a; 5. h; 6. g; 7. b; 8. d

Grammar Builder 1

Track: Lesson 1 Grammar Builder 1 (Track 2) CD: 1

GREETINGS AND PRONUNCIATION POINTS

Did you notice that there are many sounds in Arabic that don't have equivalents in English? The hardest one to master is xayn, or the letter ع, which is pronounced with a tight constriction at the very back of the throat. If you're reading the Arabic script along with the transcription, you may have noted that the shape of ع is different when it's in the middle of a word: ـعـ. But don't worry about that yet. We'll come back to that shortly. You heard the letter ع, transcribed as x, in the following words.

نَعَم	naxam	*yes*
طَبْعاً	Tabxan	*of course*
مَع السَلامَة	maxa s-salaama	*good-bye*

You also heard the letter khaa', or خ in Arabic, which is similar to *ch* in German *Bach* or Scottish *loch*. Note the word الخَيْر al-khayr in these examples.

صَباح الخَيْر	SabaaH al-khayr	*good morning*
مَساء الخَيْر	masaa' al-khayr	*good afternoon*

Arabic also has the sound h, written in Arabic as ه, which is very similar to English *h*. But don't confuse it with H, or ح in Arabic, which has much more constriction and is like the sound you make when you blow on glasses to clean them.

أَهْلاً	'ahlan	*hello*
صَباح	SabaaH	*morning*

Another common Arabic consonant is hamza, which is transcribed as an apostrophe but is written in Arabic like a small backwards 2: ء. It's a glottal stop, or the small catch in your breath when you say "uh oh." In Arabic, it's a regular consonant that comes at the beginning, at the end, or in the middle of a word.

أَهْلاً	'ahlan	*hello*
مَساء الخَيْر	masaa' al-khayr	*good afternoon*

Also note that the letters ص S, ض D, ط T, and ظ DH are pronounced with the jaw lowered, so vowels around them have a deeper sound, coming from the back of the throat. You've heard a few of these sounds.

مِن فَضْلَك	min faDlak	*please*
طَبْعاً	Tabxan	*of course*
صَباح	SabaaH	*morning*

Don't confuse them with with س s, د d, or ت t, which sound similar to the English consonants, or ذ dh, which has the sound *th* as in *this*.

Did you notice the word الـ al- in the following?

صَباح الخَيْر	SabaaH al-khayr	*good morning*
مَساء الخَيْر	masaa' al-khayr	*good afternoon*

الـ al- is the definite article in Arabic, equivalent to *the* in English. Both in writing and in pronunciation, الـ al- is a part of the word that follows it.

But الـ al- sometimes changes pronunciation. First, if the word before it ends in a vowel, the a in الـ al- will be dropped. You'll see this in transcription, but never in Arabic script.

Second, the ل l- in الـ al- is often assimilated to, or pronounced the same as, the consonant that follows it. When الـ comes before ت t-, ث th-, د d-, ذ dh-, ر r-, ز z-, س s-, ش sh-, ص S-, ض D-, ط T-, ظ DH-, and ن n-, the ل l with change into that letter in pronunciation, so instead of al-, you'll pronounce الـ as at-, ath-, ad- and so on. These are called "sun" letters, because the first letter of شَمْس shams (*sun*) is one of them. Again, this change in pronunciation will be indicated in the transcription to help you get used to it, but the spelling of الـ in Arabic doesn't change. There's an easy way to remember these letters. If you pronounce them, you'll see that your tongue is on or near your front teeth, just as in the pronunciation of the letter ل l. This similarity is what causes the change in pronunciation.

In the expression meaning *good-bye,* both of these pronunciation changes happen. The a- of al- is dropped after the -a of مَع maxa, and the l of al- is pronounced like the s- in سَلامَة salaama.

مَع السَلامَة	maxa s-salaama	*good-bye*

Here are just a few other examples of ل l in الـ changing pronunciation before "sun" letters.

الدَرْس	ad-dars	*the lesson*
الرَجُل	ar-rajul	*the man*
الشَمْس	ash-shams	*the sun*
الطَعام	aT-Taxaam	*the food*

Take It Further: Arabic Script

Included in this program is the *Guide to Arabic Script*, which will teach you everything you need to know in order to learn how to read and write Arabic. The guide is broken down into three main parts. *Part 1: Reading Arabic* introduces the Arabic alphabet in small groups of letters, explaining the different forms of each letter, with plenty of step-by-step practice reading syllables and words. *Part 2: Writing Arabic* demonstrates how to write the different forms of each letter, with similar step-by-step practice with syllables, words, and sentences. Finally, *Part 3: Reading Practice* gives you the chance to practice reading longer passages, bringing together everything that you've learned.

You can decide how and when to begin using the script guide. If your goal is simply to learn how to speak Arabic, you can stick to the transcription used in the program and work with the audio. But if you want to learn how to read and write Arabic, you should work with the script guide as well. Throughout *Essential Arabic*, you'll be directed to portions of the script guide that can be integrated into your studies. That way, you'll gradually learn how to read and write as you learn how to speak. You'll see all of the Arabic words and phrases introduced in *Essential Arabic* in both transcription and in Arabic script. You won't know all of the letters at the beginning, but you'll be able to pick out more and more letters as you learn, and soon enough you'll be reading and writing Arabic.

If you'd like to familiarize yourself with the transliteration system used in the course, you can turn to the Pronunciation and Transcription section on page 237, following the review dialogues.

Vocabulary Builder 2

Track: Lesson 1 Vocabulary Builder 2 (Track 3) CD: 1

How are you?	كَيْف الحال؟	kayf al-Haal?
Fine.	بِخَيْر.	bi-khayr.
Thank you.	شُكْراً.	shukran.
What is your name? (to a man)	ما إسْمُك؟	maa 'ismuk?
What is your name? (to a woman)	ما إسْمُكِ؟	maa 'ismuki?
My name is ...	إسْمي ...	'ismii ...
I am from ...	أَنا مِن ...	'anaa min ...
Nice to meet you.	تَشَرَّفنا.	tasharrafnaa.
Excuse me.	عَفْواً.	xafwan.
I would like ...	أُريدُ ...	'uriidu ...
With pleasure.	بِكُلِّ سُرور.	bikulli suruur.

Vocabulary Practice 2

Just like Vocabulary Practice 1, match the English in the left column with the Arabic in the right.

1. *Thank you.*
2. *Fine.*

a. بِكُلِّ سُرور bikulli suruur.
b. أُريدُ ... 'uriidu ...

3. *Excuse me.*	c. شُكْراً shukran.
4. *With pleasure.*	d. تَشَرَّفنا tasharrafnaa.
5. *What is your name? (to a woman)*	e. عَفْواً xafwan.
6. *My name is ...*	f. ما إسْمُكِ؟ maa 'ismuki?
7. *How are you?*	g. بِخَيْر bi-khayr.
8. *Nice to meet you.*	h. أنا مِن ... 'anaa min ...
9. *I am from ...*	i. ما إسْمُك؟ maa 'ismuk?
10. *I would like ...*	j. إسْمي ... 'ismii ...
11. *What is your name? (to a man)*	k. كَيْف الحال؟ kayf al-Haal?

ANSWER KEY

1. c; 2. g; 3. e; 4. a; 5. f; 6. j; 7. k; 8. d; 9. h; 10. b; 11. i

Grammar Builder 2

Track: Lesson 1 Grammar Builder 2 (Track 4) CD: 1

THE QUESTION WORD ما MAA

The word ما maa means *what?* You came across it in two important questions:

ما إسْمُك؟	maa 'ismuk?	*What's your (m.) name?*
ما إسْمُكِ؟	maa 'ismuki?	*What's your (f.) name?*

The first question is what you'd ask a man, and the second is what you'd ask a woman. Notice the different endings on إسْمُك 'ismuk and إسْمُكِ 'ismuki. These endings are the equivalent of *your*, and they're added to a noun, such as إسْم 'ism (*name*). The ending -uk is *your* (m.), -uki is *your* (f.) and -ii is *my*, whether you're a man or a woman.

إسْم	'ism	*name*
إسْمي	'ismii	*my name*
إسْمُكِ	'ismuki	*your (f.) name*
إسْمُك	'ismuk	*your (m.) name*

There are other endings for *his*, *her*, *our*, *your* (pl.), and *their*, and some of them specify gender. Arabic has singular and plural, like English, but it also has dual, which refers to two of something. So, there's a way to say *their house*, specifying that two people own the house, as opposed to *their house*, with more than two owners. But we'll come back to that later.

You also learned the pronoun أَنا 'anaa, meaning *I*, in the expression:

أَنا مِن ...	'anaa min ...	*I am from ...*

But you'll learn that pronouns are often dropped in Arabic. You saw this with the expression for *I would like*. You could say it without the pronoun, or with it:

أُريدُ ...	'uriidu ...	*I would like ...*

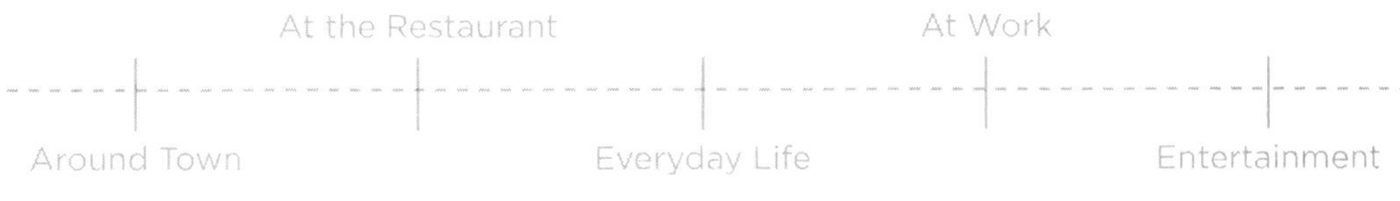

أنا أُريدُ ...	'anaa 'uriidu ...	*I would like ...*

Take It Further: Arabic Script

Now you're ready to turn to the *Guide to Arabic Script* and start learning some Arabic letters. Begin in *Part 1: Reading Arabic* with the following sections:

- The Basics
- The Arabic Alphabet
- Connecting and Non-Connecting Letters
- Group 1: Long Vowels
- Group 2: Short Vowels and Diphthongs

Then you'll be able to come back and take a closer look at some of the words you've already learned, in Arabic script.

Now that you've covered those sections in the script guide, see if you can pick out the long vowels in the following familiar words. Let's start with ا aa:

صَباح الخَيْر	SabaaH al-khayr.	*Good morning.*
مَساء الخَيْر	masaa' al-khayr.	*Good evening.*
كَيْف الحال	kayf al-Haal?	*How are you?*

You've also learned two words with ي ii and one with و uu. Can you pick them out? (Remember that Arabic letters have different shapes depending on where they appear in a word.)

إسْمي	'ismii ...	*My name is ...*
أُريدُ	'uriidu ...	*I would like ...*
بِكُلِّ سُرور	bikulli suruur.	*With pleasure.*

Now pick out the short vowels fatHa, kasra, and Damma. Don't worry about the letters that you're not familiar with yet. You'll learn them gradually.

نَعَم	naxam	*yes*
مِن فَضْلَك	min faDlak.	*Please.*
شُكْراً	shukran.	*Thank you.*
بِكُلِّ سُرور	bikulli suruur.	*With pleasure.*

And finally, look for the diphthong ay in these two phrases.

صَباح الخَيْر	SabaaH al-khayr.	*Good morning.*
كَيْف الحال	kayf al-Haal?	*How are you?*

Work Out 1

Let's do a listening comprehension exercise. Listen to the short conversation using some of the greetings and other courtesy expressions you learned in Lesson 1. As you listen, fill in the blank with the missing words, using transcription for now. The Arabic script is included; see if it helps you with the missing words as you listen and read along.

Track: Lesson 1 Work Out 1 (Track 5) CD: 1

1. ____________________

   أَهْلاً!

   Hello.

2. ____________________ **al-Haal?**

   كَيْف الحال؟

   How are you?

3. **bi-khayr,** ____________________.

   بِخَيْر، شُكْراً.

   Fine, thank you.

4. ____________________ **'ismuk?**

   ما إِسْمُك؟

   What is your name?

5. ____________________ **jaaysun.**

   إِسْمي جايسُن.

   My name is Jason.

6. ______________ **nyuu yuurk.**

أنا مِن نِيويورْك.

I am from New York.

7. ______________.

تَشَرَّفنا.

Nice to meet you.

ANSWER KEY:

1. 'ahlan; 2. kayf; 3. shukran; 4. maa; 5. 'ismii; 6. 'anaa min; 7. tasharrafnaa

---

Take It Further: Arabic Script

Earlier in this lesson you learned the basics of the Arabic alphabet, and you focused on reading long vowels, short vowels, and diphthongs. To review, see if you can match the transcription on the left to the Arabic script on the right.

1. ii / y	a. يُ
2. wa	b. وِ
3. yu	c. يَ
4. aa	d. ي
5. yaa	e. يي
6. wi	f. وَ
7. uu / w	g. يو
8. yuu	h. ا

9. yii i. و

10. ya j. يا

ANSWER KEY:

1. d, 2. f, 3. a, 4. h, 5. j, 6. b, 7. i, 8. g, 9. e, 10. c

Now you're ready to practice writing the letters that you've learned how to read. Turn to Part 2: Writing Arabic in your script guide, and go through these sections:

- Group 1: Long Vowels
- Group 2: Short Vowels and Diphthongs

Bring It All Together

Track: Lesson 1 Bring It All Together (Track 6) CD: 1

Now let's bring it all together in a conversation and add a little bit more vocabulary and structure. Read along as you listen to the following dialogue.

Samiira: *Hello!*
أَهْلاً!
'ahlan!

Jason: *Good morning!*
صَباح الخَيْر!
SabaaH al-khayr!

Samiira: *How are you?*

كَيْف الحال؟

kayf al-Haal?

Jason: *Fine, thank you.*

بِخَيْر، شُكْراً.

bi-khayr, shukran.

Samiira: *What is your name?*

ما إسْمُك؟

maa 'ismuk?

Jason: *My name is Jason.*

إسْمي جايسُن.

'ismii jaaysun.

Samiira: *Are you from America?*

أَنْتَ مِن أمريكا؟

'anta min 'amriikaa?

Jason: *Yes, I am from New York.*

نَعَم، أنا مِن نِيويورْك.

naxam, 'anaa min nyuu yuurk.

Samiira: *Are you a tourist?*

أَنْتَ سائِح؟

'anta saa'iH?

Jason: *No, I am a student.*

كَلاّ، أنا طالِب.

kallaa, 'anaa Taalib.

Samiira: *Nice to meet you, Jason.*

تَشَرَّفنا يا جايسُن.

tasharrafnaa, yaa jaaysun.

Take It Further

Track: Lesson 1 Take It Further (Track 7) CD: 1

You already knew a lot of the vocabulary used in the conversation you just heard, but let's focus on some of the new words and expressions.

أَنْتَ مِن أَمريكا؟	'anta min 'amriikaa?	*Are you from America?*
أَنْتَ سائِح؟	'anta saa'iH?	*Are you a tourist?*
كَلاّ، أنا طالِب.	kallaa, 'anaa Taalib	*No, I am a student.*

Now you know three pronouns in Arabic: أنا 'anaa (*I*), أَنْتَ 'anta (*you*, m.), and أَنْتِ 'anti (*you*, f.). Notice that there are two ways of saying *you*, depending on whether you're talking to a man or a woman.

Also notice that there are a few words missing in the Arabic sentences that you might expect to see. First, there is no present tense form of *to be* (*am, is, are*) in Arabic. And second, there is no indefinite article (*a/an*), although there is a definite article, which is ال al- (*the*).

أَنْتَ مِن نِيويورْك؟	'anta min nyuu yuurk?	*[Are] you (m.) from New York?*
أنا مِن أَمْريكا.	'anaa min 'amriikaa.	*I [am] from America.*
أَنْتَ طالِب؟	'anta Taalib?	*[Are] you (m.) [a] student?*

Take a look at يا yaa in the following sentence. It's called a vocative particle, or something that is often used when you're addressing someone directly. It comes before someone's name or title.

تَشَرَّفْنا يا جايسُن.	tasharrafnaa, yaa jaaysun.	*Nice to meet you, Jason.*

During this first lesson you learned several important expressions. Let's break some of them down and look at the meanings of the words used in them. See if you can recognize these vocabulary words in the greetings and other expressions you've seen.

صَباح	SabaaH	*morning*
مَساء	masaa'	*afternoon*
خَيْر	khayr	*blessing, good thing*
سَلام	salaam	*peace*
حال	Haal	*health, condition*
إسْم	'ism	*name*
إسْمي	'ismii	*my name*
إسْمُك	'ismuk	*your name (to a man)*
إسْمُكِ	'ismuki	*your name (to a woman)*
ما	maa	*what*
كَيْف	kayf	*how*

الـ	al-	*the*
مِن	min	*from*
مَع	maxa	*with*
بِـ	bi-	*in, at, on, with*

Work Out 2

Let's practice what you've learned throughout this first lesson. Give the Arabic translations for each of the following.

1. *Hello.* __________
2. *What's your (m) name?* __________
3. *How are you?* __________
4. *Good morning.* __________
5. *Good afternoon.* __________
6. *Please.* __________
7. *Thank you.* __________
8. *Excuse me.* __________

ANSWER KEY

1. أَهْلاً 'ahlan; 2. ما إِسْمُك maa 'ismuk?; 3. كَيْف الحال kayf al-Haal?; 4. صَباح الخَيْر SabaaH al-khayr; 5. مَساء الخَيْر masaa' al-khayr; 6. مِن فَضْلَك min faDlak; 7. شُكْراً shukran; 8. عَفْواً xafwan.

Drive It Home

Throughout this course you'll see *Drive It Home* sections that include practices on key grammar and constructions you've learned. At first glance, these exercises may seem simple and repetitive, so you may be tempted to skip them. But don't! These exercises are designed to help make the structures that you learn more automatic, and to move them into your long term memory. So take the time to do each exercise completely, writing out all the answers, and speaking them aloud to yourself. This will really help you retain the information.

First, fill in the blank with either أَنْتَ 'anta or أَنْتِ 'anti, depending on who's being addressed. The phrase مِن مِصْر min miSr means *from Egypt*, so you're asking each person, *are you from Egypt?* The names that end in -a are women's names, and the others are men's names. Don't forget to read each sentence aloud after you've written your answer.

1. yaa kariim, ______________ min miSr?

   يا كَريم، ______________ مِن مِصْر؟

2. yaa laylaa, ______________ min miSr?

   يا لَيْلى، ______________ مِن مِصْر؟

3. yaa xaadil, ______________ min miSr?

   يا عادِل، ______________ مِن مِصْر؟

4. yaa laTiifa, ______________ min miSr?

   يا لَطيفة، ______________ مِن مِصْر؟

5. yaa 'aHmad, ______________ min miSr?

   يا أَحْمَد، ______________ مِن مِصْر؟

6. yaa kamaal, ______________ min miSr?

يا كَمال، ______________ مِن مِصْر؟

ANSWERS:
1. أَنْتَ 'anta; 2, أَنْتِ 'anti; 3. أَنْتَ 'anta; 4. أَنْتِ 'anti; 5. أَنْتَ 'anta; 6. أَنْتَ 'anta

Parting Words

مَبْروك! mabruuk! *Congratulations!* You've finished your first lesson of *Essential Arabic*. How did you do? You should now be able to:

- ☐ Greet someone and ask how they're doing (Still unsure? Go back to 12)
- ☐ Be polite with helpful words like *please* and *thanks* (Still unsure? Go back to 13)
- ☐ Introduce yourself and meet other people (Still unsure? Go back to 18)
- ☐ Say other polite phrases like *Excuse me* and *I'm sorry* (Still unsure? Go back to 19)
- Use what you've learned in a short, practical conversation (Still unsure? Go back to 25)

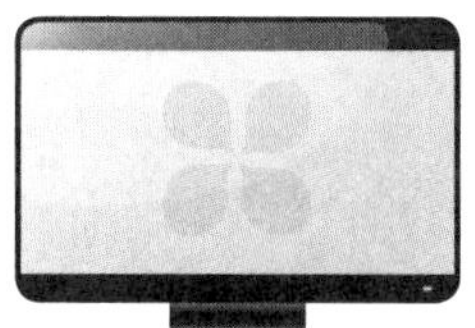

Don't forget to practice and reinforce what you've learned by visiting **www.livinglanguage.com/languagelab** for flashcards, games, and quizzes.

Take It Further

Track: Lesson 1 Take It Further (Track 8) CD: 1

Did you know that there are approximately twenty different spoken varieties of Arabic throughout the Arab World? The vocabulary you are learning here is the modern version of literary Classical Arabic, often referred to as Modern Standard Arabic (MSA), which is understood throughout the Arab World. You'll be able to get by in most situations with MSA, which is the language of commerce, the media and education used in Arabic speaking countries. But don't be surprised if you hear Egyptian Arabic, Saudi Arabic, or other local varieties used in more casual settings.

Today you've learned the basic vocabulary you need to greet people and introduce yourself. You may, of course, want to learn a few other everyday phrases, like:

حَسَناً	**Hasanan**	*all right*
شُكْراً جَزِيلاً	**shukran jaziilan**	*thanks very much*
كَفى	**kafaa**	*enough*
إلى اللِقاء	**ilaa l-liqaa'**	*so long, bye*

See you in Lesson 2!

Word Recall

You will see this section between each lesson. It gives you the chance to review key vocabulary from previous lessons, and not only the lesson you've just completed. This will reinforce the vocabulary, as well as some of the structures that you've learned so far in the course, so that they can be retained in your long-term memory. For now, though, we'll only review the key vocabulary you learned in Lesson 1.

Answer each question with the most appropriate Arabic expression, using transcription at this point.

1. *What's the opposite of* كَلاّ kalla? __________
2. *How do you greet someone in the morning?* __________
3. *How do you greet someone in the late afternoon or evening?* __________
4. *What's a more general way of greeting someone?* __________
5. *How do you say good-bye to someone?* __________
6. *How do you ask a woman what her name is?* __________
7. *How do you ask a man what his name is?* __________
8. *What do you say if someone asks you what your name is?* __________
9. *How do you ask someone how they're doing?* __________
10. *What's a polite thing to say to someone after you're introduced?* __________

ANSWERS:

1. نَعَم naxam; 2. صَباح الخَيْر SabaaH al-khayr; 3. مَساء الخَيْر masaa' al-khayr; 4. أَهْلاً 'ahlan; 5. مَعَ السَلامَة maxa s-salaama; 6. ما إِسْمُكِ؟ maa 'ismuki? 7. ما إِسْمُكَ؟ maa 'ismuk? 8. إِسْمي ... 'ismii ... 9. كَيْف الحال؟ kayf al-Haal? 10. تَشَرَّفنا tasharrafnaa.

Lesson 2: People and the Family

الدَرْس الثاني: الأشْخاص وَالعائِلة

ad-dars ath-thaanii: al-'ashkhaas wa l-xaa'ila

أهلاً 'ahlan! *Hello!* In this lesson, you'll learn how to talk about people and your family. You'll also start to learn some important points of Arabic grammar that will allow you to:

- ☐ Use general terms about people
- ☐ Use important terms about the family
- ☐ Use the plural and the dual, a special form meaning two of something
- ☐ Describe people and your family
- ☐ Put it all together in a practical conversation about the family and some occupations

But as always, let's learn some new vocabulary first. Listen to the English, and then repeat the Arabic each time you hear it. هَيّا نَبْدأ hayyaa nabda'a! *Let's begin!*

Let's start with some basic words that will come in handy in this lesson about people and the family. Again, don't worry about the Arabic script yet. We'll come to that a little later, and we'll integrate your script guide into the lesson. But scan each new word for the long and short vowels that you already know. Don't forget that و can be pronounced as long uu, or as w, and ي can be pronounced as long ii or y.

Vocabulary Builder 1

Track: Lesson 2 Vocabulary Builder 1 (Track 9) CD: 1

boy	وَلَد	walad
girl	بِنْت	bint
man	رَجُل	rajul
woman	إمْرأة	'imra'a
father	أبّ	'abb
mother	أُمّ	'umm
brother	أَخّ	'akh
sister	أُخْت	'ukht
husband	زَوْج	zawj
wife	زَوْجة	zawja
son	إبْن	'ibn
daughter	بِنْت	bint
family	عائِلة	xaa'ila

Vocabulary Practice 1

Let's review what you've just learned. First match the English word in Column A with the Arabic equivalent in Column B.

1. *woman* a. بِنْت **bint**

2. *boy* b. إِمْرأة **'imra'a**

3. *man* c. وَلَد **walad**

4. *girl* d. رَجُل **rajul**

ANSWERS:

1. b; 2. c; 3. d; 4. a

Now let's practice family terms. Find all nine family terms below, horizontally or vertically, including عائِلة **xaa'ila**.

b	*a*	*z*	*w*	*l*	*d*	*x*	*'*
i	*x*	*a*	*a*	*'*	*i*	*l*	*a*
n	*a*	*w*	*j*	*u*	*d*	*a*	*b*
w	*a*	*j*	*'*	*m*	*x*	*'*	*b*
a	*l*	*a*	*b*	*m*	*z*	*u*	*k*
l	*a*	*j*	*i*	*'*	*a*	*k*	*h*
'	*i*	*b*	*n*	*b*	*w*	*h*	*r*
z	*a*	*h*	*t*	*b*	*j*	*t*	*i*

Now fill them in below next to the Arabic script, along with their English translations:

Arabic	English
1. عائِلة	______
2. أبّ	______
3. أُمّ	______
4. أَخّ	______
5. أُخْت	______
6. زَوْج	______
7. زَوْجة	______
8. إبْن	______
9. بِنْت	______

Grammar Builder 1

Track: Lesson 2 Grammar Builder 1 (Track 10) CD: 1

GENDER AND AGREEMENT

Notice that double consonants in Arabic are pronounced with more emphasis and force than single consonants. In written Arabic script, this is marked with a shadda, like a small letter 3 on its side, written above the consonant. For example, notice the مّ in أُمّ 'umm (*mother*)

أُمّ	'umm	*mother*
أَبّ	'abb	*father*

Arabic, like many other languages, has both masculine and feminine nouns. All nouns, even ones referring to inanimate objects, are either masculine or feminine. Feminine nouns usually end in -a, which is written ة in Arabic script. But not all feminine nouns end in ة. If a noun refers to a female human, it is feminine even if it doesn't end in ة. Also, nouns referring to body parts that come in pairs are feminine, regardless of ending. Other nouns are masculine, with only a few exceptions that we'll point out.

MASCULINE NOUNS

رَجُل	rajul	*man*
وَلَد	walad	*boy*
صَباح	SabaaH	*morning*
مَساء	masaa'	*afternoon*

FEMININE NOUNS

عائِلَة	xaa'ila	*family*
إمْرأة	'imra'a	*woman*
بِنْت	bint	*girl*
يَدّ	yadd	*hand*

Many masculine nouns referring to people can be made feminine by adding the ending ة -a.

زَوْج	zawj	*husband*
زَوْجة	zawja	*wife*
طالِب	Taalib	*student (m.)*
طالِبة	Taaliba	*student (f.)*

The letter ة in Arabic is called taa' marbuuTa, or *tied t*. That's because there's a "hidden" -t in it that's pronounced in certain cases, like for example when you add a possessive ending.

زَوْجة	zawja	*wife*
زَوْجَتي	zawjatii	*my wife*

It's important to keep a noun's gender in mind when you describe things in Arabic. Adjectives agree with nouns in gender (and in a few other ways that we'll get to later). For example, the adjective كَبير kabiir means *big*, or *old* when referring to people, and when it describes a feminine noun, it takes the ending ة -a. When it describes a masculine noun, it takes no ending. Notice in the following examples that the indefinite article (*a/an*) is understood in Arabic.

رَجُل كَبير	rajul kabiir	*an old man*
إمْرأة كَبيرة	'imra'a kabiira	*an old woman*
عائِلة كَبيرة	xaa'ila kabiira	*a big family*
عائلَتي كَبيرة.	xaa'ilatii kabiira.	*My family is big.*

In the next vocabulary section, you'll see examples of the singular, the dual, and the plural in Arabic. Here's what they mean:

- Use the SINGULAR to refer to one of something.
- Use the DUAL to refer to two, or a pair, of something.
- Use the PLURAL to refer to three or more of something.

Take It Further: Arabic Script

Let's turn back to the Arabic Script Guide for a moment. In Lesson One you learned some of the basics of the Arabic alphabet, including the different forms of letters, and the fact that some letters are connectors and others are not. You also learned how to read and write both long and short vowels. In this lesson we'll focus on our first set of consonants. So turn to Part 1: Reading Arabic, and read through:

GROUP 3: ب B, ت T, AND ث TH

After you're through with Group 3, circle the letters that you recognize in the following vocabulary that you've learned so far.

بِنْت (**bint**, *girl/daughter*)	أَبّ (**'abb**, *father*)
أُخْت (**'ukht**, *sister*)	إبْن (**'ibn**, *son*)
كَبير (**kabiir**, *big*)	صَباح (**SabaaH**, *morning*)
أَنْتَ (**'anta**, *you, [m.]*)	أَنْتِ (**'anti**, *you, [f.]*)

Vocabulary Builder 2

Track: Lesson 2 Vocabulary Builder 2 (Track 11) CD: 1

boy (m. sg.)	وَلَد	walad
two boys (m. du.)	وَلَدان	waladaan
boys (m. pl.)	أَوْلاد	'awlaad
teacher (m. sg.)	مُدَرِّس	mudarris
two teachers (m. du.)	مُدَرِّسان	mudarrisaan
teachers (m. pl.)	مُدَرِّسون	mudarrisuun
girl (f. sg.)	بِنْت	bint
two girls (f. du.)	بِنْتان	bintaan
girls (f. pl.)	بَنات	banaat
teacher (f. sg.)	مُدَرِّسَة	mudarrisa
two teachers (f. du.)	مُدَرِّسَتان	mudarrisataan
teachers (f. pl.)	مُدَرِّسات	mudarrisaat
family (f. sg.)	عائِلَة	xaa'ila
two families (f. du.)	عائِلَتان	xaa'ilataan
families (f. pl.)	عائِلات	xaa'ilaat
two big families (f. du.)	عائِلَتان كَبيرَتان	xaa'ilataan kabiirataan
big families (f. pl.)	عائلات كَبيرَة	xaa'ilaat kabiira

Vocabulary Practice 2

How do you say the following words in Arabic?

1. *family* ____________
2. *boy* ____________
3. *male teacher* ____________
4. *girl* ____________
5. *female teacher* ____________

ANSWERS:

1. عائِلَة xaa'ila; 2. وَلَد walad; 3. مُدَرِّس mudarris; 4. بِنْت bint; 5. مُدَرِّسَة mudarrisa

Now match the singular forms of each word in the left column with the plural forms in the right column, and then translate. We'll talk more about singulars, plurals, and duals in the next section.

1. بِنْت bint	a. أَوْلاد 'awlaad
2. عائِلَة xaa'ila	b. مُدَرِّسون mudarrisuun
3. مُدَرِّسة mudarrisa	c. بَنات banaat
4. وَلَد walad	d. عائِلات xaa'ilaat
5. مُدَرِّس mudarris	e. مُدَرِّسات mudarrisaat

ANSWER KEY

1. c (*girl/girls*); 2. d (*family/families*); 3. e (*female teacher/teachers*); 4. a (*boy/boys*); 5. b (*male teacher/teachers*)

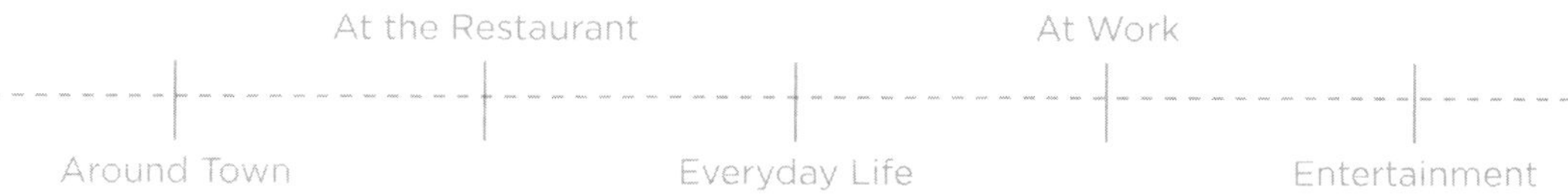

Grammar Builder 2

Track: Lesson 2 Grammar Builder 2 (Track 12) CD: 1

THE DUAL AND THE PLURAL

As you can see from the last vocabulary list, Arabic has a special way of talking about a pair of something, called the dual form, as well as a plural form, which is used to talk about three or more of something. The dual is formed regularly, by adding ـان -aan to the end of a singular noun.

وَلَد	walad	*(a) boy*
وَلَدان	waladaan	*two boys*
بِنْت	bint	*(a) girl*
بِنْتان	bintaan	*a pair of girls*
عائِلة	xaa'ila	*(a) family*
عائِلَتان	xaa'ilataan	*two families*

Notice that the "hidden t" of ة is pronounced and converted into a ت taa' in writing when the dual ending is added to عائِلة xaa'ila (*family*).

To talk about more than two of something, use the plural. Arabic has both a regular and an irregular plural. The regular plural is formed by adding ـون -uun to masculine nouns, and ـات -aat to feminine nouns, which replaces the feminine singular ending ة a.

مُدَرِّس	mudarris	*male teacher*
مُدَرِّسون	mudarrisuun	*male teachers*
مُدَرِّسة	mudarrisa	*female teacher*
مُدَرِّسات	mudarrisaat	*female teachers*

But most Arabic nouns have irregular plurals. To understand how they're formed, take a look at the noun وَلَد walad (*boy*). Like most Arabic words, it contains three root consonants: و-ل-د w-l-d. The three root consonants of most typical Arabic words can be thought of as a skeleton, and the meaning of the word is changed by deleting or changing the vowels that come before, after, or between the consonants of that skeleton. This happens not only to nouns, but also to verbs and adjectives, extending meaning in a whole range of ways that we'll cover gradually.

This type of irregular noun plural is often called a "broken" plural, because the noun is "broken" apart, and vowels are added, deleted, or rearranged. There are patterns that broken plurals follow, but they're unpredictable, so it's really best to simply memorize the plural of each noun that you learn. So far, you've only learned two irregular or broken plurals.

وَلَد	walad	*boy*
أَوْلاد	'awlaad	*boys*
بِنْت	bint	*girl*
بَنات	banaat	*girls*

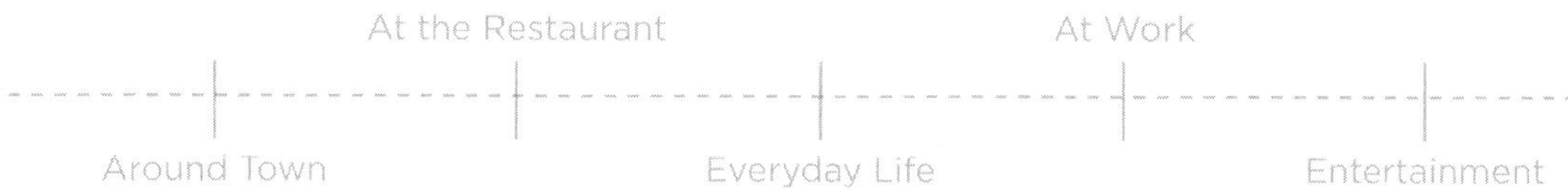

As for the adjectives, we mentioned earlier that they must agree in gender with, or match, the noun they're describing. They also match the noun in number. Take a look at these examples:

رَجُل كَبير	rajul kabiir	*(a) big/old man*
عائِلة كَبْيرة	xaa'ila kabiira	*(a) big family*
عائِلَتان كَبْيرَتان	xaa'ilataan kabiirataan	*two big families*
عائِلات كَبيرة	xaa'ilaat kabiira	*big families*

The basic form of the adjective *big* is كَبير kabiir. This is the form that you use to describe a masculine singular noun, such as رَجُل rajul (*man*). To form the feminine singular, just add ة -a, as in كَبْيرة kabiira.

To form the dual, add ـان -aan to the end of the masculine adjective, so it becomes كبيران kabiiraan. To put the feminine form of the adjective كبيرة kabiira into the dual, change theة into a ت taa' before adding the ـان -aan to the end, so that it becomes كَبيرتان kabiirataan.

Did you notice that the same singular form, كَبيرة kabiira, is used with both the singular عائِلَة xaa'ila and the plural عائِلات xaa'ilaat? That's because the feminine singular form of the adjective is used with non-human plural nouns, including animals, cars, houses, tables, and so on. For example, *big houses* is بُيوت كبيرة buyuut kabiira.

But when an adjective is used with a noun that refers to people, like مُدَرِّسات mudarrisaat (*[female] teachers*), it has to be in the feminine plural form, مُدَرِّسات

جَيِّدات mudarrisaat jayyidaat (*good teachers*). We'll come back to masculine human plurals later.

Work Out 1

Track: Lesson 2 Work Out 1 (Track 13) CD: 1

Let's do a listening comprehension exercise to review some of what you've just learned. Listen to the audio, and fill in the blanks with the missing words. Then give the complete translations. When you're through, listen to this exercise a second time, focusing only on the Arabic script. See how many letters you can make out as you read.

1. walad / ____________ / 'awlaad

   وَلَد / وَلَدان / أَوْلاد

2. ____________ / bintaan / banaat

   بِنْت / بِنْتان / بَنات

3. mudarris / mudarrisaan / ____________

   مُدَرِّس / مُدَرِّسان / مُدَرِّسون

4. mudarrisa / ____________ / mudarrisaat

   مُدَرِّسَة / مُدَرِّسَتان / مُدَرِّسات

5. xaa'ila kabiira / xaa'ilataan kabiirataan / ____________

   عائِلَة كَبيرَة / عائِلَتان كَبيرَتان / عائِلات كَبيرَة

6. rajul ____________

   رَجُل كَبير

7. mudarrisa ______________

مُدَرِّسة جَيِّدة

8. ______________ jayyidaat

مُدَرِّسات جَيِّدات

9. al-______________ wa l-______________ mudarrisaan.

الأَبّ وَالأَخّ مُدَرِّسان.

10. al-______________ wa l-______________ mudarrisataan jayyidataan.

الأُمّ وَالأُخْت مُدَرِّستان جَيِّدتان.

ANSWER KEY

1. waladaan (*boy, two boys, boys*); 2. bint (*girl, two girls, girls*); 3. mudarrisuun (*male teacher, two male teachers, male teachers*); 4. mudarrisataan (*female teacher, two female teachers, female teachers*); 5. xaa'ilaat kabiira (*a big family, two big families, big families*); 6. kabiir (*a big/old man*); 7. jayyida (*a good female teacher*); 8. mudarrisaat (*good female teachers*); 9. 'abb, 'akh (*The father and the brother are teachers.*) 10. 'umm, 'ukht (*The mother and the sister are good teachers.*)

Bring It All Together

Track: Lesson 2 Bring It All Together (Track 14) CD: 1

Now let's bring it all together and add a little bit more vocabulary and structure. Read along as you listen to Ahmad talking about himself. Repeat the Arabic in the pauses provided.

إسْمي أَحْمَد.	'ismii 'aHmad.	*My name is Ahmad.*
أَنا دُكتور.	'anaa duktuur.	*I am a doctor.*

عائِلَتي كَبيرَة.	xaa'ilatii kabiira.	*My family is big.*
هَذِه زَوْجَتي.	haadhihi zawjatii.	*This is my wife.*
زَوْجَتي مُدَرِّسة.	zawjatii mudarrisa.	*My wife is a teacher.*
لَدَيْنا بِنْت وَوَلَدان.	ladaynaa bint wa waladaan.	*We have a girl and two boys.*
هَذِه أُمّي.	haadhihi 'ummii.	*This is my mother.*
أُمّي أَيْضاً مُدَرِّسة.	'ummii 'ayDan mudarrisa.	*My mother is a teacher too.*
زَوْجَتي وَأُمّي مُدَرِّستان.	zawjatii wa 'ummii mudarrisataan.	*My wife and my mother are (both) teachers.*
أَبي مُهَنْدِس.	'abbii muhandis.	*My father is an engineer.*
هَذِه أُخْتي مَرْيَم وَأَخي مُصْطَفى وَأَخي الصَغير فاروق.	haadhihi 'ukhtii, maryam, wa 'akhii muSTafa wa 'akhii aS-Saghiir faaruuq.	*This is my sister, Mariam, my brother Mustafa, and my little brother, Farouk.*
مَرْيَم وَمُصْطَفى وَفاروق طُلّاب.	Maryam wa muSTafa wa faaruuq Tullaab.	*Mariam, Mustafa, and Farouk are students.*

Take It Further

Track: Lesson 2 Take It Further (Track 15) CD: 1

You most likely understood most of the words and phrases in this segment, but there were also some new ones. You probably guessed that دُكْتور duktuur means *doctor* and that مُهَنْدِس muhandis means *engineer*. Can you guess what the feminine form of مُهَنْدِس muhandis is? Yes, that's right – مُهَنْدِسة muhandisa. And have you spotted لَدَيْنا ladaynaa, the useful word you can use to say *we have*? The word و wa (*and*) is also useful to know. You must have guessed that هَذِهِ haadhihi means *this* in هَذِه زَوْجَتي haadhihi zawjatii (*this is my wife*). You'll learn more demonstratives in the coming lessons. Finally, صَغير Saghiir means *little* or *small*, أَيْضاً 'ayDan means *also*, and طُلاّب Tullaab (*students*) is the plural of طالِب Taalib (*student*).

Remember, there is no equivalent of the verb *to be* and its present tense forms, such as *am* or *is*, in Arabic.

أَنا دُكْتور.	'anaa duktuur.	*I'm a doctor.*
أَبي مُهَنْدِس.	'abii muhandis.	*My father is an engineer.*
عائِلَتي كَبيرة.	xaa'ilatii kabiira.	*My family is big.*

Most of the vocabulary in this lesson has focused on people and the family, but you've also learned some useful general vocabulary as well. Let's review it here.

كَبير	kabiir	*big, old (people)*
صَغير	Saghiir	*small, young (people)*
جَيِّد	jayyid	*good*
طالِب	Taalib	*student, (m.)*
طُلاّب	Tullaab	*students, (m. or mixed)*
طالِبة	Taaliba	*student, (f.)*

طالِبات	Taalibaat	*students, (f.)*
أَيْضاً	'ayDan	*also, too, as well*
هَذِهِ	haadhihi	*this, (f.)*
لَدَيْنا	ladayna	*we have*

You've already learned a few broken plurals: أَوْلاد 'awlaad (*boys*), بَنات banaat (*girls*), and طُلّاب Tullaab (*students*). Let's look at the plurals of a few more nouns that you know already. Can you pick out the root consonants in both the singular and plural forms?

رَجُل/رِجال	rajul/rijaal	*man/men*
إمْرأة/نِساء	'imra'a/nisaa'	*woman/women*
أَبّ/آباء	'abb/'aabaa'	*father/fathers*
أُمّ/أُمَّهات	'umm/'ummahaat	*mother/mothers*
أَخّ/إخْوَة	'akh/'ikhwa	*brother/brothers*
أُخْت/أَخَوات	'ukht/'akhawaat	*sister/sisters*
زَوْج/أَزْواج	zawj/'azwaaj	*husband/husbands*
إبْن/أَبْناء	'ibn/'abnaa'	*son/sons*
إسْم/أَسْماء	'ism/'asmaa'	*name/names*

Notice that نِساء nisaa' (*women*) is really an irregular plural, since it doesn't use the same skeleton as the singular form.

Work Out 2

Let's practice what you've learned. Match the Arabic expressions in Column A with the English equivalents in Column B.

1. وَلَد walad	a. *woman*
2. أُمّي 'ummii	b. *sister*
3. إِمْرَأَة 'imra'a	c. *girls*
4. رَجُل rajul	d. *two men*
5. أُخْت 'ukht	e. *my mother*
6. أَخّ 'akh	f. *wives*
7. بَنات banaat	g. *families*
8. رَجُلان rajulaan	h. *boy*
9. زَوْجات zawjaat	i. *brother*
10. عائِلات xaa'ilaat	j. *man*

ANSWER KEY

1. h; 2. e; 3. a; 4. j; 5. b; 6. i; 7. c; 8. d; 9. f; 10. g

Now answer each question, following the example below. Don't worry about the grammar behind these possessive phrases yet. We'll come back to that later.

'ibn 'ummii (*my mother's son*) = 'akhii (*my brother*)

إِبْن أمّي

1. **zawj 'ummii** (*my mother's husband*) = ____________

زَوْج أُمّي

2. **zawjat 'abbii** (*my father's wife*) = ____________

زَوْجَة أَبي

3. **'akhuu 'ukhtii** (*my sister's brother*) = ____________

أَخو أُخْتي

4. **bint 'abbii** (*my father's daughter*) = ____________

بِنْت أَبي

ANSWER KEY

1. أَبي **'abbii**; 2. أُمّي **'ummii**; 3. أخي **'akhii**; 4. أُخْتي **'ukhtii**.

Take It Further: Arabic Script

Now you're ready to practice writing the letters that you've learned how to read. Turn to *Part 2: Writing Arabic* in your script guide, and go through this section:

- Group 3: ب, ت, and ث

Drive It Home

Now let's help move some of what you've learned into your long term memory with some exercises. Remember that even though they seem simple, they'll help make some key constructions more automatic, so take the time to do these exercises completely.

First, make a phrase with each of the following masculine nouns and the adjective كَبير kabiir (*big, old*). Then translate your answers.

1. وَلَد walad ____________________
2. رَجُل rajul ____________________
3. أَبّ 'abb ____________________
4. أَخّ 'akh ____________________
5. زَوْج zawj ____________________
6. إبْن 'ibn ____________________

ANSWERS KEY:

1. وَلَد كَبير walad kabiir (*a big/old boy*); 2. رَجُل كَبير rajul kabiir (*a big/old man*); 3. أَبّ كَبير 'abb kabiir (*a big/old father*); 4. أَخّ كَبير 'akh kabiir (*a big/old brother*); 5. زَوْج كَبير zawj kabiir (*a big/old husband*); 6. إبْن كَبير 'ibn kabiir (*a big/old son*)

Now do the same with these feminine nouns.

1. بِنْت bint ____________________
2. إمْرَأة 'imra'a ____________________
3. أُمّ 'umm ____________________
4. أُخْت 'ukht ____________________
5. زَوْجَة zawja ____________________
6. عائِلة xaa'ila ____________________

ANSWERS:

1. بِنْت كَبْيرة bint kabiira (*a big/old girl/daughter*); 2. إمْرَأة كَبْيرة 'imra'a kabiira (*a big/old woman*); 3. أُمّ كَبْيرة 'umm kabiira (*a big/old mother*); 4. أُخْت كَبْيرة 'ukht kabiira (*a big/old sister*); 5. زَوْجَة كَبْيرة zawja kabiira (*a big/old wife*); 6. عائِلة كَبْيرة xaa'ila kabiira (*a big family*)

Parting Words

You've learned a lot of new vocabulary and important constructions in this lesson. Now you can:

- ☐ Use general terms about people (Still unsure? Go back to 35)
- ☐ Use important terms about the family (Still unsure? Go back to 37)
- ☐ Use the plural and the dual, a special form meaning two of something (Still unsure? Go back to 41)
- ☐ Describe people and your family (Still unsure? Go back to 43)
- ☐ Put it all together in a practical conversation about the family and some occupations (Still unsure? Go back to 47)

Don't forget to practice and reinforce what you've learned by visiting **www.livinglanguage.com/languagelab** for flashcards, games, and quizzes.

Take It Further

Track: Lesson 2 Take It Further (Track 16) CD: 1

Here are a few more vocabulary words that will come in handy for talking about the family.

جَدّة	jadda	*grandmother*
جَدّ	jadd	*grandfather*
حَفيدة	Hafiida	*granddaughter*
حَفيد	Hafiid	*grandson*
خال	khaal	*maternal uncle*
عَمّ	xamm	*paternal uncle*
خالَة	khaala	*maternal aunt*
عَمَّة	xamma	*paternal aunt*

يَوْماً سَعيداً yawman saxiidan *Have a wonderful day!* See you in Lesson 3.

Word Recall

Once again, you'll see this section between each lesson. Remember that it will give you the chance to review some key vocabulary from all the preceding lessons, so now we'll look at what you've learned in Lessons 1 and 2.

Can you remember what these Arabic words and phrases mean?

1. أب **'abb** ______
2. كَبير **kabiir** ______
3. زَوْجة **zawja** ______
4. كَلاّ **kallaa** ______
5. صَباح الخَيْر **SabaaH al-khayr** ______
6. إمْرَأة **'imra'a** ______
7. كَيْف الحال؟ **kayf al-Haal** ______
8. صَغير **Saghiir** ______
9. رَجُل **rajul** ______
10. حَفيد **Hafiid** ______
11. أُخْتي **'ukhtii** ______
12. طالِب **Taalib** ______
13. عائِلَة **xaa'ila** ______
14. إسمي **'ismii** ______
15. نَعَم **naxam** ______

ANSWER KEY

1. *father*; 2. *big*; 3. *wife*; 4. *no*; 5. *good morning*; 6. *woman*; 7. *How are you?*; 8. *small*; 9. *man*; 10. *grandson*; 11. *my sister*; 12. *student*; 13. *family*; 14. *my name*; 15. *yes*

Lesson 3: Numbers

الدرْس الثالِث: الأَرْقام

ad-dars ath-thaalith: al-'arqaam

كَيْف الحال؟ **kayf al-Haal?** *How are you?* Are you ready for more Arabic? This lesson is all about numbers and counting. You'll learn how to:

- □ count from one to ten
- □ use lower numbers to count people and things
- □ count from eleven to nineteen
- □ use those numbers to count people and things
- □ practice more with numbers, and use higher numbers

We'll get right to it with basic numbers. هَيّا نَبْدَأ **hayyaa nabda'a.** *Let's begin.*

Vocabulary Builder 1

Track: Lesson 3 Vocabulary Builder 1 (Track 17) CD: 1

zero	صِفر	**Sifr**
one	واحِد	**waaHid**
two	إثْنان	**'ithnaan**
three	ثَلاثة	**thalaatha**

four	أَرْبَعة	'arbaxa
five	خَمْسة	khamsa
six	سِتّة	sitta
seven	سَبْعَة	sabxa
eight	ثَمانية	thamaaniya
nine	تِسْعَة	tisxa
ten	عَشَرَة	xashara

Vocabulary Practice 1

Let's review what you've just learned. Give the next number in each sequence. The entire sentence is written in Arabic script. Does that help you remember the answers?

1. واحِد إثْنان ثَلاثة

   waaHid 'ithnaan ________________

2. سِتّة سَبْعَة ثَمانية

   sitta sabxa ________________

3. ثَلاثة أَرْبَعة خَمْسة

   thalaatha 'arbaxa ________________

4. ثَمانية تِسْعَة عَشَرَة

   thamaaniya tisxa ________________

5. خَمْسة سِتَّة سَبْعَة

khamsa sitta ________________

ANSWERS:

1. thalaatha; 2. thamaaniya; 3. khamsa; 4. xashara; 5. sabxa

Now let's do a little basic arithmetic.

1. واحِد + إثْنان = ثلاثة

waahid + 'ithnaan = ________________

2. سَبْعَة - ثَلاثة = أَرْبَعة

sabxa – 'thalaatha = ________________

3. سِتَّة + إثْنان = ثَمانِية

sitta + 'ithnaan = ________________

4. عَشَرَة - خَمْسة = خَمْسة

xashara – khamsa = ________________

5. سَبْعَة + ثَلاثة - أَرْبَعة = سِتَّة

sabxa + thalaatha – 'arbaxa = ________________

ANSWERS:

1. thalaatha; 2. 'arbaxa; 3. thamaaniya; 4. khamsa; 5. sitta

Grammar Builder 1

Track: Lesson 3 Grammar Builder 1 (Track 18) CD: 1

COUNTING THINGS: ONE THROUGH TEN

Take a closer look at the numbers you've just learned. Did you notice that the ending on إِثْنان 'ithnaan is the same as the dual ending you learned in the last lesson, ـان -aan? This makes a lot of sense, since the meaning of the dual is *two* of something.

When you're simply counting from one to ten, using only numbers, you use the forms that you learned in Vocabulary Builder 1. Numbers have different written forms in Arabic than they do in English:

0	٠
1	١
2	٢
3	٣
4	٤
5	٥
6	٦
7	٧
8	٨
9	٩
10	١٠

But getting back to the spoken language, if you're counting people or things, there are a couple of points that you need to keep in mind about Arabic.

The number واحِد **waaHid** (*one*) is only used for emphasis. Remember that the indefinite article *a/an* is understood in Arabic, so a noun on its own such as وَلَد **walad** already carries the meaning *a boy*, which basically means *one boy*. If you want to emphasize one and only one, use واحِد after the noun.

وَلَد	**walad**	*a boy*
وَلَد واحِد	**walad waaHid**	*one and only one boy*

Because Arabic has a dual form (the ending ـان **-aan**), you don't have to use the number إثْنان **'ithnaan** to specify two of something. Just use the dual form.

وَلَدان	**waladaan**	*two boys*
بِنْتان	**bintaan**	*two girls*

Things get a bit more complicated when counting between three and ten of something. You use the plural form of the noun, but the number itself disagrees in gender with that noun. If it's a masculine noun, use the same forms of ثَلاثة **thalaatha** (*three*) through عَشَرة **xashara** (*ten*) that you learned in Vocabulary Builder 1. You can tell that they're feminine forms, because they all end in ة. And remember that since the number and the noun disagree in gender, it's these feminine forms you'll use with masculine plural nouns. One small thing to keep in mind, though, is that the "hidden t" of ة will be pronounced on the number.

ثَلاثة طُلّاب	thalaathat Tullaab	*three students (m.)*
أَرْبَعة أوْلاد	'arbaxat 'awlaad	*four boys*
خَمْسَة رِجال	khamsat rijaal	*five men*

When counting between three and ten feminine nouns, use the feminine plural forms with the masculine forms of the numbers you learned. As you can probably imagine, in many cases, all you need to do is take off the feminine ending ة on the numbers ثَلاثة thalaatha (*three*) through عَشَرَة xashara (*ten*) to form the masculine. But there are a few minor variations, so we'll take a look at all the masculine forms here.

ثَلاث	thalaath	*three (m.)*
أَرْبَع	'arbax	*four (m.)*
خَمْس	khams	*five (m.)*
سِتّ	sitt	*six (m.)*
سَبَع	sabax	*seven (m.)*
ثَماني	thamaanii	*eight (m.)*
تِسَع	tisax	*nine (m.)*
عَشَر	xashar	*ten (m.)*

Note that خَمْس khams may also be pronounced khamas. Now let's see how that works when counting feminine nouns.

ثَلاث طالِبات	thalaath Taalibaat	*three students (f)*
أَرْبَع بَنات	'arbax banaat	*four girls*
خَمْس نِساء	khams nisaa'	*five women*

Later in this lesson we'll look at the numbers eleven through nineteen.

Take It Further: Arabic Script

Ready to learn another three Arabic letters? Turn to your script guide, Part 1: Reading Arabic, and read:

- Group 4: ج j, ح H, and خ kh

When you're through with Group 4, take a look at the following words, all of which you've learned by now, and see if you can recognize all the vowels, as well as the consonants ب b, ت t, ث th, ج j, ح H, and خ kh. Don't forget to look for initial, medial, final, and isolated forms, and keep in mind that the vowels ي ii and و uu are also pronounced as the consonants y and w.

1. ثَلاثة (thalaatha, *three*)
2. خَيْر (khayr, *blessing*)
3. صَباح (SabaaH, *morning*)
4. عَفْواً (xafwan, *excuse me*)
5. حال (Haal, *condition, state*)
6. رَجُل (rajul, *man*)
7. بَنات (banaat, *girls*)
8. زَوْجَتي (zawjatii, *my wife*)
9. أَبْناء ('abnaa', *sons*)
10. طُلّاب (Tullaab, *students*)
11. أُخْت ('ukht, *sister*)
12. إِخْوة ('ikhwa, *brothers*)

Vocabulary Builder 2

Track: Lesson 3 Vocabulary Builder 2 (Track 19) CD: 1

eleven	أَحَدَ عَشَر	'aHada xashar
twelve	إثنا عَشَر	'ithnaa xashar
thirteen	ثَلاثَة عَشَر	thalaathata xashar
fourteen	أَرْبَعة عَشَر	'arbaxata xashar
fifteen	خَمْسَة عَشَر	khamsata xashar
sixteen	سِتّة عَشَر	sittata xashar
seventeen	سَبْعة عَشَر	sabxata xashar
eighteen	ثَمانية عَشَر	thamaaniyata xashar
nineteen	تِسْعة عَشَر	tisxata xashar

Vocabulary Practice 2

Let's practice those higher numbers. What number follows each of these sequences?

1. إثنا عَشَر 'ithnaa xashar, ثَلاثَة عَشَر thalaathata xashar, ____________
2. سِتّة عَشَر sittata xashar, سَبْعة عَشَر sabxata xashar, ____________
3. ثَلاثَة عَشَر thalaathata xashar, أَرْبَعة عَشَر 'arbaxata xashar, ____________
4. تِسْعَة tisxa, عَشَرَة xashara, ____________
5. أَرْبَعة عَشَر 'arbaxata xashar, خَمْسَة عَشَر khamsata xashar, ____________

ANSWER KEY

1. أَرْبعة عَشَر 'arbaxata xashar; 2. ثَمانية عَشَر thamaaniyata xashar; 3. خَمْسة عَشَر khamsata xashar; 4. أَحَدَ عَشَر 'aHada xashar; 5. سِتّة عَشَر sittata xashar

Now let's do a little basic arithmetic. See if you're able to read the answers in Arabic script.

1. waaHid + 'ithnaa xashar = ____________________

واحِد + إثنا عَشَر = ثَلاثة عَشَر

2. sabxata xashar – 'thalaatha = ____________________

سَبْعة عَشَر - ثَلاثة = أَرْبَعة عَشَر

3. sittata xashar + 'ithnaan = ____________________

سِتّة عَشَر + إثْنان = ثَمانية عَشَر

4. tisxata xashar – khamsa = ____________________

تِسْعة عَشَر - خَمْسة = أَرْبَعة عَشَر

5. sabxata xashar + thalaatha – 'arbaxa = ____________________

سَبْعة عَشَر + ثَلاثة - أَرْبَعة = سِتّة عَشَر

ANSWER KEY:

1. thalaathata xashar; 2. 'arbaxata xashar; 3. thamaaniyata xashar; 4. 'arbaxata xashar; 5. sittata xashar

Grammar Builder 2

Track: Lesson 3 Grammar Builder 2 (Track 20) CD: 1

COUNTING THINGS: ELEVEN THROUGH NINETEEN

Now you know how to count as high as تِسْعَة عَشَر tisxata xashar (*nineteen*). Remember that with the numbers from ثَلاثة thalaatha (*three*) through عَشَرَة xashara (*ten*), the noun is in the plural form, but the number itself takes the opposite gender. With أَحَدَ عَشَر 'aHada xashar (*eleven*) through تِسْعَة عَشَر tisxata xashar (*nineteen*), the rules in very formal Arabic are a bit complex, so we'll focus on the less formal, and much simpler, spoken Arabic you're likely to hear.

The only surprise is that the noun will be in the singular form, in fact not just for أَحَدَ عَشَر 'aHada xashar (*eleven*) through تِسْعَة عَشَر tisxata xashar (*nineteen*), but for numbers even higher, which we'll get to later. But in informal Arabic, you don't need to worry about any gender mismatch.

ثَلاثَة عَشَر وَلَد	thalaathata xashar walad	*thirteen boys*
ثَلاثَة عَشَر بِنْت	thalaathata xashar bint	*thirteen girls*
تِسْعة عشر سائِح	tisxata xashar saa'iH	*nineteen male tourists*
تِسعَة عَشَر سائِحة	tisxata xashar saa'iHa	*nineteen female tourists*

Notice that even though the phrases refer to plural boys, girls, and tourists, the nouns وَلَد walad (*boy*), بِنْت bint (*girl*), سائِح saa'iH (*male tourist*), and سائِحة saa'iHa (*female tourist*) are all singular.

Work Out 1

Track: Lesson 3 Work Out 1 (Track 21) CD: 1

Listen to your audio to put everything you've learned together and to give yourself a work out using Arabic numbers. Fill in the blanks with the missing words that you hear.

1. *three men* — ثَلاثة رِجال thalaathat ________
2. *three women* — ثَلاث نِساء ________ nisaa'
3. *four men* — أَرْبَعة رِجال ________ rijaal
4. *four women* — أَرْبَع نِساء 'arbax ________
5. *five men* — خَمْسة رِجال ________ rijaal
6. *five women* — خَمَس نِساء ________ nisaa'
7. *six men* — سِتّة رِجال ________ rijaal
8. *six women* — سِتّ نِساء ________ nisaa'
9. *seven men* — سَبْعَة رِجال ________ rijaal
10. *seven women* — سَبَع نِساء ________ nisaa'
11. *eight men* — ثَمانيَة رِجال ________ rijaal
12. *eight women* — ثَماني نِساء ________ nisaa'

13. *nine men* تِسْعة رِجال ______ rijaal

14. *nine women* تِسَع نِساء ______ nisaa'

15. *ten men* عَشَرة رِجال ______ rijaal

16. *ten women* عَشَر نِساء ______ nisaa'

ANSWER KEY

1. rijaal; 2. thalaath; 3. 'arbaxat; 4. nisaa'; 5. khamsat; 6. khamas; 7. sittat; 8. sitt; 9. sabxat; 10. sabax; 11. thamaaniyat; 12. thamaanii; 13. tisxat; 14. tisax; 15. xasharat; 16. xashar

Bring It All Together

Track: Lesson 3 Bring It All Together (Track 22) CD: 1

Let's count from 20 to 90.

عِشرون	xishruun	*twenty*
ثلاثون	thalaathuun	*thirty*
أرْبعون	'arbaxuun	*forty*
خَمسون	khamsuun	*fifty*
سِتّون	sittuun	*sixty*
سَبْعون	sabxuun	*seventy*
ثَمانون	thamaanuun	*eighty*
تِسعون	tisxuun	*ninety*

Luckily, the tens do not have separate forms for masculine and feminine; the same form is used with either gender. The ones are joined with the tens by وَ wa (*and*). Also, unlike in English, the ones precede the tens in all two-digit numbers above twenty.

واحِد وَثَلاثون	waaHid wa thalaathuun	*thirty-one*
سِتّة وَثمانون	sitta wa thamanuun	*eighty-six*

Work Out 2

First, translate the following numbers from Arabic into English. We'll bring back written Arabic digits to help you practice recognizing them.

1. thalaatha ٣ __________
2. sabxuun ٧٠ __________
3. thalaatha wa xishruun ٢٣ __________
4. tisxa ٩ __________
5. xashara ١٠ __________
6. khamsa wa sittuun ٦٥ __________
7. thalaatha wa khamsuun ٥٣ __________
8. thamaaniya wa tisxuun ٩٨ __________
9. sitta wa sittuun ٦٦ __________
10. waaHid wa 'arbaxuun ٤١ __________

ANSWER KEY

1. 3; 2. 70; 3. 23; 4. 9; 5. 10; 6. 65; 7. 53; 8. 98; 9. 66; 10. 41

Now translate the following numbers into Arabic. Spell the numbers out in transcription.

1. *6* __________
2. *57* __________
3. *64* __________
4. *50* __________
5. *34* __________
6. *90* __________
7. *85* __________
8. *27* __________
9. *20* __________
10. *0* __________

ANSWER KEY

1. sitta; 2. sabxa wa khamsuun 3. 'arbaxa wa sittuun; 4. khamsuun; 5. 'arbaxa wa thalaathuun; 6. tisxuun; 7. khamsa wa thamaanuun; 8. sabxa wa xishruun; 9. xishruun; 10. Sifr

Drive It Home

Let's practice counting both masculine and feminine plural nouns. Fill in each of the following blanks with أَوْلاد 'awlaad (*boys*), and read the sentence aloud, paying close attention to the ending on the number.

1. ثَلاثة thalaathat ______
2. أَرْبَعة 'arbaxat ______
3. خَمْسة khamsat ______
4. سِتّة sittat ______
5. سَبْعَة sabxat ______
6. ثَمانِية thamaaniyat ______
7. تِسْعَة tisaxat ______
8. عَشَرَة xasharat ______

ANSWER KEY:

1. thalaathat 'awlaad (*three boys*); 2. 'arbaxat 'awlaad (*four boys*), and so on.

Now do the same with بَنات banaat (*girls*).

1. ثَلاث thalaath ______
2. أَرْبَع 'arbax ______
3. خَمَس khamas ______
4. سِتّ sitt ______
5. سَبَع sabax ______

6. ثَماني **thamaanii** ______________

7. تِسَع **tisax** ______________

8. عَشَر **xashar** ______________

ANSWER KEY:

1. thalaath banaat (*three girls*); 2. 'arbax banaat (*four girls*), and so on.

Take It Further: Arabic Script

Now let's practice writing the three letters you learned how to read earlier. Turn to your script guide, Part 2: Writing Arabic, and do:

- Group 4: ح ,ج, and خ

Parting Words

You've focused mostly on numbers in this lesson, so now you should know how to:

- ☐ Count from one to ten (Still unsure? Go back to 57.)
- ☐ Use lower numbers to count people and things (Still unsure? Go back to 60.)
- ☐ Count from eleven to nineteen (Still unsure? Go back to 64.)
- ☐ Use those numbers to count people and things (Still unsure? Go back to 66.)
- ☐ Use higher numbers (Still unsure? Go back to 68.)

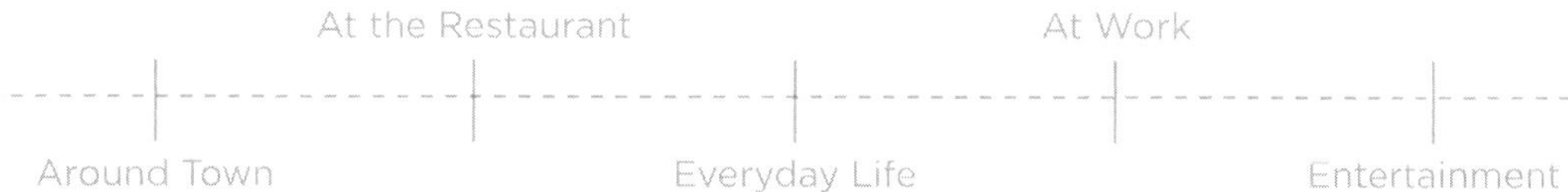

Don't forget to practice and reinforce what you've learned by visiting **www.livinglanguage.com/languagelab** for flashcards, games, and quizzes.

Take It Further

Track: Lesson 3 Take It Further (Track 23) CD: 1

Here are a few higher numbers in Arabic.

مِئة	mi'a	*one hundred*
مِئتان	mi'ataan	*two hundred*
ثلاثُمِئة	thalaathumi'a	*three hundred*
أَلْف	'alf	*one thousand*
مِليون	milyuun	*one million*

Let's take a second look at written Arabic numbers. Did you know that Arabic numerals are actually of Indian origin? And the numerals used in English are of Arabic origin! عالَم صَغير xaalam Saghiir! *It's a small world!* Here again are the numerals used in Arabic, with some suggestions on how to remember them.

0	٠	*0 is just a dot, not an open circle.*
1	١	*This is easy enough, just a stroke similar to 1.*
2	٢	*This looks like a 2 on its side.*

3	٣	*This looks just like a 3 on its side, but with a longer tail.*
4	٤	*This looks like a backwards 3.*
5	٥	*Be careful. This is 5, not 0.*
6	٦	*Be careful. This looks like a 7, but it's a 6.*
7	٧	*Think of the v in the word seven.*
8	٨	*Just invert the 7 to get 8.*
9	٩	*Easy enough.*
10	١٠	*A 1 followed by a 0, just like in English.*

Keep in mind that even though Arabic words are written right-to-left, Arabic numbers are written left-to-right.

45	٤٥
210	٢١٠
367	٣٦٧

Word Recall

As always, let's do a cumulative review of the most important vocabulary you've learned so far, from Lessons 1 through 3. Match the words and phrases in English with their Arabic equivalents.

1. *grandfather* — a. صِفر Sifr
2. *family* — b. أَهْلاً 'ahlan
3. *student (f.)* — c. إثنا عَشَر وَلَد 'ithnaa xashar walad
4. *men* — d. رِجال rijaal
5. *thirty* — e. خَمَس نِساء khamas nisaa'
6. *teacher (m.)* — f. صَباح الخَيْر SabaaH al-khayr
7. *five women* — g. كَيْف الحال kayf al-Haal
8. *the mother's son* — h. كَبير kabiir
9. *How are you?* — i. إبْن الأُم 'ibn al-'umm
10. *zero* — j. طالِبة Taaliba
11. *small* — k. ثلاثون thalaathuun
12. *Good morning.* — l. عائِلة xaa'ila
13. *big* — m. مُدَرِّس mudarris
14. *twelve boys* — n. جَدّ jadd
15. *Hello.* — o. صَغير Saghiir

ANSWER KEY

1. n; 2. l; 3. j; 4. d; 5. k; 6. m; 7. e; 8. i; 9. g; 10. a; 11. o; 12. f; 13. h; 14. c; 15. b

Lesson 4: Around the House

الدَرْس الرابِع: حَوْل البَيْت

ad-dars ar-raabix: Hawl al-bayt

مَرْحَباً! **marhaban!** *Welcome!* Lesson 4 will introduce you to some basic vocabulary related to the home and everyday life. You will:

- ☐ Learn basic vocabulary related to rooms in a house
- ☐ Use simple sentences to speak about the home
- ☐ Learn a few basic verbs
- ☐ Put them to use to talk about everyday activities
- ☐ Learn some adjectives that you can use to describe your house

Let's get started with some basic words and phrases.

Vocabulary Builder 1

Track: Lesson 4 Vocabulary Builder 1 (Track 24) CD: 2

house	بَيْت	**bayt**
(he) lives	يَسْكُن	**yaskun**
Ahmad lives in the house.	يَسْكُن أحْمَد في البَيْت.	**yaskun 'aHmad fi l-bayt.**
room	غُرْفَة	**ghurfa**

There are five rooms in Ahmad's house,	فِي بَيْت أحْمَد خَمْس غُرَف	fii bayt 'aHmad khams ghuraf,
and two bedrooms,	وَغُرْفتا نَوْم	wa ghurfataa nawm,
and a living room,	وَغُرْفَة جُلوس	wa ghurfat juluus,
and a dining room,	وَغُرْفة طَعام	wa ghurfat Taxaam,
and a study,	وغُرْفة مَكْتَب	wa ghurfat maktab.
and there is a kitchen, of course,	وَهُناك مَطْبَخ طبعاً	wa hunaka maTbakh Tabxan
and a bathroom,	وَحَمّام	wa Hammaam,
and a pretty garden, too.	وَحَديقة جَميلة أيضا.	wa Hadiiqa jamiila 'ayDan.

Vocabulary Practice 1

Can you remember what these words mean? Write the equivalent in English:

1. غُرْفة مَكْتَب ghurfat maktab ____________
2. مَطْبَخ maTbakh ____________
3. جَميلة jamiila ____________
4. حَديقة Hadiiqa ____________
5. غُرْفَة جُلوس ghurfat juluus ____________
6. حَمّام Hammaam ____________
7. بَيْت bayt ____________

8. غُرَف ghuraf ____________

9. غُرْفة نَوْم ghurfat nawm ____________

10. يَسْكُن yaskun ____________

ANSWER KEY

1. *office*; 2. *kitchen*; 3. *pretty, beautiful*; 4. *garden*; 5. *living room*; 6. *bathroom*; 7. *house*; 8. *rooms*; 9. *bedroom*; 10. *(he) lives*

Grammar Builder 1

Track: Lesson 4 Grammar Builder 1 (Track 25) CD: 1

THE إضافة 'IDAAFA CONSTRUCTION

The names of many of the rooms in a house are examples of a very common construction in Arabic known as إضافة 'iDaafa. These constructions are simply possessive noun phrases (*a/the X of a/the Y*, or *the Y's X* in English), but their formation in Arabic is a bit different from what you might expect. Take a look at some examples.

غُرْفَة جُلوس	ghurfat juluus	*a living room*
غُرْفة طَعام	ghurfat Taxaam	*a dining room*
غُرْفة مَكْتَب	ghurfat maktab	*a study*

You can recognize that the first word in each of these examples, غُرْفَة ghurfa, means *room*. Literally, غُرْفَة جُلوس ghurfat juluus means *a room of sitting*, غُرْفة طَعام ghurfat Taxaam means *a room of food*, and غُرْفة مَكْتَب ghurfat maktab means something like *a room of writing*. So each of these phrases is an X of Y construction, and they're all examples of an indefinite إضافة 'iDaafa, meaning simply *a room* and not *the room*. To form an indefinite إضافة 'iDaafa, just string the two nouns together, and imagine that there's an invisible *of* in Arabic. One important thing to keep in mind, though, is that the "hidden t" of ة will be pronounced if the first noun ends in ة, as is the case with غُرْفَة ghurfa.

There are also definite إضافة 'iDaafa in Arabic, and the only difference is that the definite article will appear before the second noun only. Arabic never allows the definite article before the first noun in an إضافة 'iDaafa, even though it's interpreted as definite. Let's see some examples

غُرْفة النَوْم	ghurfat an-nawm	*the bedroom*
غُرْفة الطَعام	ghurfat aT-Taxaam	*the dining room*
غُرْفة المَكْتَب	ghurfat al-maktab	*the study*

Of course, إضافة 'iDaafa constructions are not limited to the names of rooms! They can be used to express all sorts of possessive relationships. Just remember that if the definite article appears before the second noun, both nouns are interpreted as definite (*the*). If there is no definite article, both nouns are interpreted as indefinite (*a/an*).

إسم الوَلَد	'ism al-walad	*the boy's name/ the name of the boy*

بَيْت الرَّجُل	bayt ar-rajul	*the man's house/ the house of the man*
بَيْت رَجُل	bayt rajul	*a man's house/ a house of a man*
كِتاب بِنْت	kitaab bint	*a girl's book/ a book of a girl*

Also, take a look at the words مَكْتَب maktab (*office*) and مَطْبَخ maTbakh (*kitchen*). The prefix مَـ ma- is something you'll see a lot in Arabic, and it sometimes implies that the noun is the name of a place. These words literally mean *place of writing* (an office or study, or a desk) and *place of cooking* (a kitchen).

You also saw the verb يَسكُن yaskun (*live*). We'll go over verbs later, but for now let's get acquainted just with the basics. The form يَسكُن yaskun literally means *he lives*. It's got a prefix, يَـ ya-, which is part of the conjugation for هوَ huwa, or *he*. Sometimes you'll hear it with a final -u, يَسكُنُ yaskunu but that's often dropped in spoken Arabic.

Just like most Arabic nouns, the majority of Arabic verbs are constructed from three basic root consonants, in this case س-ك-ن s-k-n. You've already seen the roots of a few other verbs, for example in مَكْتَب maktab (*office, place of writing*), and غُرفة الجُلوس ghurfat al-juluus (*living/sitting room*). The root consonants for *write* are ك-ت-ب k-t-b, and the ones for *sit* are ج-ل-س j-l-s. So we can take those roots and produce the verb forms:

هو يَكْتُب	huwa yaktub	*he writes*
هو يَجْلِس	huwa yajlis	*he sits*

But don't worry yet about what goes on with the vowels in between the root consonants. We'll come to that later. For now, just get used to the idea of picking out root consonants in Arabic, and that basic meanings are extended from them in a whole variety of ways. This will come in very handy, as it's really the heart of the Arabic language!

Finally, notice that sentences in Arabic can begin either with a verb or with a noun. And in the second example below, don't forget that there is no word corresponding to *am*, *is*, or *are*; it's simply understood.

يَسْكُن أحْمَد في البَيْت.	yaskun 'aHmad fi-l bayt.	*Ahmad lives in the house.*
الحَديقة جَميلة.	al-Hadiiqa jamiila.	*The garden [is] pretty.*

Take It Further: Arabic Script

Let's return to the script guide and cover another group of Arabic letters. Go to Part 1: Reading Arabic, and go through:

- Group 5: د d, ذ dh, ر r, and ز z

After you're done with Group 5, take a look at the following familiar words. By now you can recognize all the vowels, as well as the consonants ب b, ت t, ث th, ج j, ح H, خ kh, د d, ذ dh, ر r, and ز z.

1. هَذِهِ (haadhihi, *this, f.*)
2. سُرور (suruur, *pleasure*)
3. شُكْراً (shukran, *thank you*)
4. أُريد ('uriid, *I would like/I want*)
5. سائِح (saa'iH, *tourist*)
6. تَشَرَّفْنا (tasharrafnaa, *nice to meet you*)
7. أَوْلاد ('awlaad, *boys*)
8. زَوْجَتي (zawjatii, *my wife*)
9. مُدَرِّس (mudarris, *teacher*)
10. بَيْت (bayt, *house*)

Vocabulary Builder 2

Track: Lesson 4 Vocabulary Builder 2 (Track 26) CD: 1

(he) sleeps	يَنام	yanaam
Ahmad sleeps.	يَنام أحْمَد.	yanaam 'aHmad.
Mona sleeps.	تَنام مُنى.	tanaam munaa.
(he) eats	يَأكُل	ya'kul
Ahmad eats.	يأكُل أحْمَد.	ya'kul 'aHmad.
Mona eats.	تَأْكُل مُنى.	ta'kul munaa.
(he) sits	يَجْلِس	yajlis
Ahmad sits.	يَجْلِس أحْمَد.	yajlis 'aHmad.
Mona sits.	تَجْلِس مُنى.	tajlis munaa.
bed	سَرير	sariir
dining table	مائِدَة	maa'ida
chair	مَقْعَد	maqxad

Vocabulary Practice 2

Translate the following English words and phrases into Arabic, using transcription. The Arabic script is given with the English. Can you recognize enough letters by now so that it helps you remember the answers? But there's a catch; the sentences may be either subject-first or verb-first. You'll need to look at the Arabic script to help you figure out how you're supposed to answer.

1. *(he) sits* يَجْلِس
2. *Mona eats.* تَأْكُل مُنى.
3. *dining table* مائدة
4. *chair* مَقْعَد
5. *Ahmad sits.* أحْمَد يَجْلِس.
6. *bed* سَرير
7. *(he) eats* يَأكُل
8. *Mona sleeps.* مُنى تَنام.

ANSWER KEY

1. yajlis; 2. ta'kul munaa. 3. maa'ida; 4. maqxad; 5. 'aHmad yajlis. 6. sariir; 7. ya'kul; 8. munaa tanaam

Grammar Builder 2

Track: Lesson 4 Grammar Builder 2 (Track 27) CD: 1

INTRODUCTION TO VERBS

Let's talk a bit about Arabic verbs now. You'll be happy to know that there are only two basic tenses in Arabic, the perfect, or past, referring to completed actions; and the imperfect, or the present, used to refer to actions taking place now or actions that happen generally. (In case you're wondering, the future tense is really simple; it's just the present with a little prefix-like particle in front of it!).

Arabic verbs, like verbs in many languages, change form depending on who or what is doing the action. In the present tense, both prefixes and suffixes are added to the verb stem, which is formed from the three root consonants that we mentioned earlier. These prefixes and suffixes vary according to the subject.

For instance, in the present tense, the prefix يَـ ya- is added for the هوَ huwa (*he*) form, and the prefix تَـ ta- is added for the هيَ hiya (*she*) form. Remember that Arabic sentences can have two different orders: SV (subject ... verb ...) or VS (verb ... subject ...). If the subject is a name or a noun, the verb may come first. Let's see some examples of that with verbs that you've learned.

يَأكُل أَحْمَد.	ya'kul 'aHmad	*Ahmad eats/is eating*
تَأكُل مُنى.	ta'kul munaa	*Mona eats/is eating*
يَجْلِس أحْمَد.	yajlis 'aHmad	*Ahmad sits/is sitting*
تَجْلِس مُنى.	tajlis munaa	*Mona sits/is sitting*

You can see the root consonants plainly enough in ج-ل-س j-l-s (*sit*). Notice that the hamza, or the glottal stop that we're representing as an apostrophe in transcription, can be part of a root or stem: ء-ك-ل '-k-l (*eat*).

For the أنا 'anaa (*I*) form, verbs carry the prefix 'a-, and for the أَنْتَ 'anta (*you*, m.) and أَنْتِ 'anti (*you*, f.) forms, they carry the prefix تَـ ta-. But notice that the أَنْتِ 'anti (*you*, f.) form also has a suffix: ين -iin.

أنا أَجْلِس.	'anaa 'ajlis	*I sit/am sitting*
أنْتَ تَجْلِس.	'anta tajlis	*you (m.) sit/are sitting*
أَنْتِ تَجْلِسين.	'anti tajlisiin	*you (f.) sit/are sitting*

The يَـ ya- prefix is also used for the dual *they*, when you're talking about just two people, as well as the plural *they*, for three or more people. The dual *they* ending is ـان -aan, and the plural *they* ending is ـون -uun.

مُنى وَأَحْمَد يَجْلِسان.	munaa wa 'aHmad yajlisaan.	*Mona and Ahmad are sitting.*
مُنى وَأَحْمَد وَمُصْطفى يَجْلِسون.	muna wa 'aHmad wa muSTafaa yajlisuun.	*Mona, Ahmad, and Mustafa are sitting.*

The form for نَحْنُ naHnu (*we*) takes the prefix نَـ na-. The plural form أَنْتُم 'antum (*you, all of you, you all*) takes the same prefix as the singular أَنْتَ 'anta and أَنْتِ 'anti, that is, تَـ ta- but it also has the ending ـون -uun.

نَحْنُ نَجْلِس	naHnu najlis	*we sit / are sitting*
أَنْتُم تَجْلِسون	'antum tajlisuun	*all of you sit / are sitting*

There are just a couple of other verb forms that we'll come back to later, but this is a very good start! Let's summarize the present tense conjugation.

You'll sometimes see the short vowel ending Damma ُ u on the present tense forms for أنا 'anaa (*I*), أَنْتَ 'anta (*you, m.*), أَنْتِ 'anti (*you, f.*), هوَ huwa (*he*), هيَ hiya (*she*), and نَحنُ naHnu (*we*). Note, though, that they're often dropped in spoken Arabic.

PRONOUN	PREFIX	SUFFIX	EXAMPLE: SIT
'anaa (*I*) أنا	'a- أ	—/-u	'ajlis أَجْلِس
'anta (*you, m.*) أَنْتَ	ta- تَـ	—/-u	tajlis تَجْلِس
'anti (*you, f.*) أَنْتِ	ta- تَـ	-iin ين	tajlisiin تَجْلِسين
huwa (*he*) هوَ	ya- يَـ	—/-u	yajlis يَجْلِس
hiya (*she*) هيَ	ta- تَـ	—/-u	tajlis تَجْلِس
naHnu (*we*) نَحنُ	na- نَـ	—/-u	najlis نَجْلِس

PRONOUN	PREFIX	SUFFIX	EXAMPLE: SIT
'antum (*you, pl.*) أَنْتُم	ta- تَـ	-uun ون	tajlisuun تَجْلِسون
humaa (*the two of them*) هُما	ya- يَـ	-aan ان	yajlisaan يَجْلِسان
hum (*they*) هُم	ya- يَـ	-uun ون	yajlisuun يَجْلِسون

Work Out 1

Track: Lesson 4 Work Out 1 (Track 28) CD: 1

Let's practice verbs. Listen to your recordings, and fill in the prefix that you hear. Again, see if the Arabic script can help you remember.

1. *I sit* — أنا أَجْلِس
   'anaa ______________ jlis
2. *you (m.) sit* — أَنْتَ تَجْلِس
   'anta ______________ jlis
3. *you (f.) sit* — أَنْتِ تَجْلِسين
   'anti ______________ jlisiin
4. *he sits* — هوَ يَجْلِس
   huwa ______________ jlis

5. *she sits* — هيَ تَجْلِس
hiya ________________ jlis

6. *we sit* — نَحنُ نَجْلِس
naHnu ________________ jlis

7. *all of you sit* — أَنْتُم تَجْلِسون
'antum ________________ jlisuun

8. *the two of them sit* — هُما يَجْلِسان
humaa ________________ jlisaan

9. *they sit* — هُم يَجْلِسون
hum ________________ jlisuun

ANSWER KEY

1. أَ 'a; 2. تَـ ta; 3. تَـ ta; 4. يَـ ya; 5. تَـ ta; 6. نَـ na; 7. تَـ ta; 8. يَـ ya; 9. يَـ ya

Bring It All Together

Track: Lesson 4 Bring It All Together (Track 29) CD: 3

Now let's bring it all together in a dialogue and add a little bit more vocabulary.

أَسْكُن في بيتي مَعَ زَوْجَتي مُنى.	'askun fii baytii maxa zawjatii, munaa.	*I live in my house with my wife, Mona.*
بَيْتُنا جَديد.	baytunaa jadiid.	*Our house is new.*
هُناك خَمَس غُرَف في البَيْت.	hunaaka khamas ghuraf fi l-bayt.	*There are five rooms in the house.*

هُناكَ شُرْفة كَبيرة في غُرْفة النَوم.	hunaaka shurfa kabiira fii ghurfat an-nawm.	*There is a large window in the bedroom.*
الشُرْفة تُطِلّ على الحَديقة.	ash-shurfa tuTill xala l-Hadiiqa.	*The window looks out onto the garden.*
أثاثُنا جَديد.	'athaathunaa jadiid.	*Our furniture is new.*
مائِدة الطَعام جَديدة.	maa'idat aT-Taxaam jadiida.	*The dining table is new.*
أَدَوات المَطْبَخ جَديدة أيضاً.	'adawaat al-maTbakh jadiida 'ayDan.	*The kitchen utensils are new, too.*
لَكِن أثاث غُرْفَة الجُلوس قَديم.	laakin 'athaath ghurfat al-juluus qadiim.	*But the living room furniture is old.*
أَوْلادُنا يُحِبّون البَيْت الجَديد.	'awlaadunaa yuHibbuun al-bayt al-jadiid.	*Our children love the new house.*
البَيْت كَبير وَمُشْمِس وَقَريب مِن مَدْرَسَتِهِم.	al-bayt kabiir wa mushmis, wa qariib min madrasatihim.	*The house is big, sunny, and near their school.*

Take It Further

Track: Lesson 4 Take It Further (Track 30) CD: 3

Let's look at some of the new vocabulary that you heard in Bring It All Together.

يَسْكُن	yaskun	*he lives*

يُحِبّ	yuHibb	*he loves*
شُرْفَة	shurfa	*window*
أَثاث	'athaath	*furniture*
جَديد	jadiid	*new*
قَديم	qadiim	*old*
مَدْرَسة	madrasa	*school*
مُشْمِس	mushmis	*sunny*
قَريب	qariib	*near, close by*
قَريب مِن	qariib min	*near, close to (something)*
في	fii	*in*
مَعَ	maxa	*with*
لَكِن	laakin	*but*

Back in Lesson 1 you learned that you can add suffixes to nouns, such as إسْم 'ism (*name*) to express *my* and *your*.

إسْمي	'ismii	*my name*
إسْمُك	'ismuk	*your (m.) name*
إسْمُكِ	'ismuki	*your (f.) name*

You came across a few other possessive suffixes like these in the Bring It All Together section.

ـنا	-naa	*our*
بَيتُنا	baytunaa	*our house*
أثاثُنا	'athaathunaa	*our furniture*
ـهُم	-hum	*their*
مَدْرَسَتُهُم	madrasatuhum	*their school*

Now let's take a closer look at describing things. Do you remember from Lesson 2 that adjectives like كَبير kabiir (*big, old*) agree with the nouns they describe? If the noun is masculine, the adjective is as well, and if the noun in feminine, you simply add ة -a to make the adjective feminine.

رَجُل كَبير	rajul kabiir	*an old man*
إمْرأة كَبيرة	'imra'a kabiira	*an old woman*

Now you've seen a few more examples of this. The nouns بَيْت bayt (*house*) and أثاث 'athaath (*furniture*) are both masculine, so جَديد jadiid (*new*) is masculine as well, with no ending.

بَيْتُنا جَديد.	baytunaa jadiid.	*Our house is new.*
أَثاثُنا جَديد.	'athaathunaa jadiid.	*Our furniture is new.*

But the noun مائِدة maa'ida (*table*) in the phrase مائدة الطَعام maa'idat aT-Taxam (*dining table*) is feminine, so جَديد jadiid (*new*) has to agree with it by taking the ending ة -a.

مائدة الطَعام جَديدة	maa'idat aT-Taxam jadiida.	*The dining table is new.*

If you want to describe any plural that is not a human being - *dogs, tables, houses, computers*, etc. - the adjective will take feminine singular agreement. You saw this with أَدَوات 'adawaat (*utensils*). Notice the ending on جَديدَة jadiida (*new*).

أدَوات المَطْبَخ جَديدة أيْضاً.	'adawaat al-maTbakh jadiida 'ayDan.	*The kitchen utensils are new, too.*

Finally, there's one more important point to mention about using descriptive words in Arabic. Not only do they have to agree in gender, but they also agree in definiteness with the noun they modify. So, if the noun is definite, so is the adjective, with the same definite article الـ al- added to the beginning. The same pronunciation changes apply.

وَلَد صَغير	walad Saghiir	*a little boy*
الوَلَد الصَغير	al-walad aS-Saghiir	*the little boy*
بِنْت صَغيرة	bint Saghiira	*a little girl*
البِنْت الصَغيرة	al-bint aS-Saghiira	*the little girl*

You've seen an example of this already. Notice that البَيْت al-bayt (*the house*) is masculine and definite, so is الجَديد al-jadiid (*new*) as well.

أَولادُنا يُحِبّون البَيْت الجَديد.	'awlaadunaa yuHibbuun al-bayt al-jadiid.	*Our children love the new house.*

Work Out 2

Let's practice what you've learned in this lesson. Complete each sentence with the correct form of يَسْكُن yaskun (*lives*), and then translate your answers.

1. أنا ________ في البَيْت.

'anaa ________ fii l-bayt.

2. مُنى وَأَحْمَد وَطارِق ________ في بَيْت كَبير.

munaa wa 'aHmad wa Taariq ________ fii bayt kabiir.

3. أنْتَ ________ في بَيْت صَغير.

'anta ________ fii bayt Saghiir.

4. أبي ________ مَعَ أُختي.

'abii ________ maxa 'ukhtii.

5. نَحْن ________ في بَيْت كبير.

naHnu ________ fii bayt kabiir.

6. مُحَمَّد ________ في بَيْت صَغير.

muHammad ________ fii bayt Saghiir.

7. في بَيْت كبير. ______ مُنى

munaa ______ fii bayt kabiir.

8. في بَيْت كَبير. ______ أنا وَزَوْجَتي

'anaa wa zawjatii ______ fii bayt kabiir.

9. مَعَ أُختي. ______ الأولاد

al-'awlaad ______ maxa 'ukhtii.

10. في بَيْت صَغير. ______ البِنْت

al-bint ______ fii bayt Saghiir.

ANSWER KEY

1. أَسْكُن 'askun (*I live in the house.*) 2. يَسْكُنون yaskunuun (*Mona and Ahmad and Tariq live in a big house.*) 3. تَسْكُن taskun (*You live in a small house.*) 4. يَسْكُن yaskun (*My father lives with my sister.*) 5. نَسْكُن naskun (*We live in a big house.*) 6. يَسْكُن yaskun (*Mohammed lives in a small house.*) 7. تَسْكُن taskun (*Mona lives in a big house.*) 8. نَسْكُن naskun (*My wife and I live in a big house.*) 9. يَسْكُنون yaskunuun (*The children live with my sister.*) 10. تَسْكُن taskun (*The girl lives in a small house.*)

And let's practice describing things as well. Fill in each blank with the correct form of the adjective in parentheses, and then translate the phrases. Remember to use the ending ة- -a when describing all feminine singular nouns, as well as any non-human plurals. Also, don't forget to use the definite article when describing definite nouns.

1. (كَبير) ______ رَجُل

rajul ______ (kabiir)

2. (جَديد) ______ البَيْت

al-bayt ______ (jadiid)

3. (كبير) ____________ إمْرأة

'imra'a ____________ (kabiir)

4. (كبير) ____________ الإمْرأة

al-'imra'a ____________ (kabiir)

5. (جَديد) ____________ أدَوات

'adawaat ____________ (jadiid)

6. (قَريب) ____________ مَدْرَسة

madrassa ____________ (qariib)

7. قديم ____________ الأثاث

al-'athaath ____________ (qadiim)

8. (مُشْمِس) ____________ غُرْفة

ghurfa ____________ (mushmis)

9. (جَديد) ____________ المَدْرَسة

al-madrassa ____________ (jadiid)

10. (صَغير) ____________ المائدة

al-maa'ida ____________ (Saghiir)

ANSWER KEY

1. كبير kabiir (*a big/old man*); 2. الجَديد al-jadiid (*the new house*); 3. كَبيرة kabiira (*a big/old woman*); 4. الكَبيرة al-kabiira (*the big/old woman*); 5. جَديدة jadiida (*new utensils*); 6. قَريبة qariiba (*a nearby school*); 7. القديم al-qadiim (*the old furniture*); 8. مُشْمِسة mushmisa (*a sunny room*); 9. الجَديدة al-jadiida (*the new school*); 10. الصَغيرة aS-Saghiira (*the small table*)

Drive It Home

Let's do some more practice with verbs, to really help you remember the forms. First, fill in the correct forms of يَفْعَلُ yafxalu (*does*). Use the short Damma ending for practice.

1. أنا 'anaa ______________
2. أَنْتَ 'anta ______________
3. أَنْتِ 'anti ______________
4. هوَ huwa ______________
5. هيَ hiya ______________
6. نَحنُ naHnu ______________
7. أَنْتُم 'antum ______________
8. هُما humaa ______________
9. هُم hum ______________

ANSWER KEY

1. أَفْعَلُ 'afxalu (*I do*); 2. تَفْعَلُ tafxalu (*you, m., do*); 3. تَفْعَلِين tafxaliin (*you, f. do*); 4. يَفْعَلُ yafxalu (*he does*); 5. تَفْعَلُ tafxalu (*she does*); 6. نَفْعَلُ nafxalu (*we do*); 7. تَفْعَلُونْ tafxaluun (*you, pl., do*); 8. يفْعَلاَن yafxalaan (*they, dual, do*); 9. يَفْعَلُون yafxaluun (*they, pl., do*).

Now let's try it once more with يَدْرُسُ yadrusu (*studies*). Remember that the practice and repetition will help you remember these forms!

1. أنا 'anaa ______________
2. أَنْتَ 'anta ______________

3. أَنْتِ 'anti ______________________

4. هوَ huwa ______________________

5. هيَ hiya ______________________

6. نَحنُ naHnu ______________________

7. أَنْتُم 'antum ______________________

8. هُما humaa ______________________

9. هُم hum ______________________

ANSWER KEY

1. أَدْرُسُ 'adrusu (*I study*); 2. تَدْرُسُ tadrusu (*you, m., study*); 3. تَدْرُسِين tadrusiin (*you, f., study*); 4. يَدْرُسُ yadrusu (*he studies*); 5. تَدْرُسُ tadrusu (*she studies*); 6. نَدْرُسُ nadrusu (*we study*); 7. تَدْرُسُون tadrusuun (*you, pl., study*); 8. يَدْرُسَان yadrusaan (*they, dual, study*); 9. تَدْرُسَون yadrusuun (*they study*).

Take It Further: Arabic Script

Let's return to the script guide and practice writing the letters you learned how to read earlier in this lesson. Go to Part 2: Writing Arabic, and go through:

- Group 5: ر, ذ, د, and ز

Parting Words

In this lesson, you learned a lot of important grammar that's useful for talking about your home and everyday life. You should know how to:

□ Use basic vocabulary related to rooms in a house (Still unsure? Go back to 76.)

- ☐ Form simple sentences about the home (Still unsure? Go back to 78.)
- ☐ Use a few basic verbs (Still unsure? Go back to 82.)
- ☐ Put them to use to talk about everyday activities (Still unsure? Go back to 84.)

  Use some descriptive terms that you can use to describe your house (Still unsure? Go back to 88.)

Don't forget to practice and reinforce what you've learned by visiting **www.livinglanguage.com/languagelab** for flashcards, games, and quizzes.

Take It Further

Track: Lesson 4 Take It Further (Track 31) CD: 1

رائع raa'ix! *Wonderful!* Now you know enough Arabic words to describe the rooms in your house. You may of course want to talk about the other parts of your house or building:

مَدْخَل	madkhal	*entrance*
الطابِق	aT-Taabiq	*the floor*
غُرْفة الضُيوف	ghurfat aD-Duyuuf	*the guest room*
المِصْعَد	al-miSxad	*the elevator*

إلى اللِقاء 'ilaa l-iqaa'! *So long!*

Word Recall

Can you match the Arabic script and transcription with the English translation?

1. المِصْعَد al-miSxad — a. *students*
2. البَيْت al-bayt — b. *he eats*
3. حَمّام Hammaam — c. *wife*
4. طُلاّب Tullaab — d. *the house*
5. ثمانية عَشَر thamaaniyata xashar — e. *thank you*
6. يَأكُل ya'kul — f. *the elevator*
7. زَوْجة zawja — g. *teacher (m.)*
8. كَيْف الحال kayf al-Haal — h. *names*
9. شُكْراً shukran — i. *big (m.)*
10. رَجُل rajul — j. *a bathroom*
11. مُدَرِّس mudarris — k. *small (f.)*
12. أَسْماء 'asmaa' — l. *woman*
13. صَغيرة Saghiira — m. *eighteen*
14. كَبير kabiir — n. *man*
15. إمْرأة 'imra'a — o. *How are you?*

ANSWER KEY

1. f; 2. d; 3. j; 4. a; 5. m; 6. b; 7. c; 8. o; 9. e; 10. n; 11. g; 12. h; 13. k; 14. i; 15. l

Lesson 5: Describing Things

الدَرْس الخامِس: وَصْف الأشياء

ad-dars al-khaamis: waSf al-ashyaa'

أهلاً وَسَهْلاً **'ahlan wa sahlan!** *Welcome!* This lesson will focus on talking about your surroundings, so you'll:

- ☐ Review pronouns, and learn a few new ones
- ☐ Learn how to use them with some more basic descriptive terms
- ☐ Learn the words for everyday objects and colors
- ☐ Use words like *this* and *these*
- ☐ Put it all to use in sentences that bring together a lot of what you've been learning

هَيّا نَبْدَأْ حالاً **hayyaa nabda' Haalan!** Let's begin right away! As always, we'll start with some basic words that will come in handy.

Vocabulary Builder 1

Track: Lesson 5 Vocabulary Builder 1 (Track 1) CD: 2

I	أَنا	**'anaa**
you (to a man)	أَنْتَ	**'anta**
you (to a woman)	أَنْتِ	**'anti**

he	هُوَ	huwa
she	هِيَ	hiya
we	نَحْنُ	naHnu
you (to men, or a mixed group)	أَنْتُم	'antum
you (to women)	أَنْتُنَّ	'antunna
they (for men or a mixed group)	هُم	hum
they (for women)	هُنَّ	hunna
tall	طَويل	Tawiil
happy	سَعيد	saxiid

Vocabulary Practice 1

Which pronoun would you use to talk ...

1. *to your friend Layla?* ________
2. *about yourself?* ________
3. *about your friends Layla, Mariam, and Latifa?* ________
4. *to your friend Ahmad?* ________
5. *about yourself and two of your friends?* ________
6. *to your friends Mariam, Ahmad, and Mahmoud?* ________

7. *about your friend Layla?* ________________

8. *about your friend Ahmad?* ________________

9. *to your friends Mariam, Layla, and Latifa?* ________________

10. *about your friends Mariam, Ahmad, and Mahmoud?* ________________

ANSWER KEY:
1. أَنْتِ 'anti; 2. أَنا 'anaa; 3. هُنَّ hunna; 4. أَنْتَ 'anta; 5. نَحْنُ naHnu; 6. أَنْتُم 'antum; 7. هِيَ hiya; 8. هُوَ huwa; 9. أَنْتُنَّ 'antunna; 10. هُم hum

Grammar Builder 1

Track: Lesson 5 Grammar Builder 1 (Track 2) CD: 2

ADJECTIVE AGREEMENT WITH PLURALS

Let's take a look at some simple sentences using those pronouns with descriptive adjectives like طويل Tawiil (*tall*), سعيد saxiid (*happy*), and تعيس taxiis (*sad*). Remember that the verb *to be* doesn't exist in the affirmative present tense in Arabic, so in a sentence like *you are tall*, the adjective follows the pronoun directly, and agrees with it in gender and number.

أَنا طَويل.	'anaa Tawiil.	*I am tall. (m.)*
أنا طَويلة.	'anaa Tawiila.	*I am tall. (f.)*
أَنْتَ طَويل.	'anta Tawiil.	*You are tall. (m.)*
أَنْتِ طَويلة.	'anti Tawiila.	*You are tall. (f.)*
هوَ سَعيد.	huwa saxiid.	*He is happy.*

هيَ سَعيدة.	hiya saxiida.	*She is happy.*

Now let's talk about plurals. Remember that هُم **hum** (*they*) is used when talking about groups of three or more men, or about mixed groups, and هُنَّ **hunna** (*they*) is used when talking about groups of three or more women. To talk to or about two people, there are special dual pronouns in Arabic, أَنْتُما **'antumaa** (*the two of you, you two*) and هُما **humaa** (*the two of them, those two*), but we'll come back to the dual later.

Remember that adjectives agree with the nouns they describe not only in gender, but also in number. So, if you want to say *we are happy*, *they are happy*, or *you (pl.) are happy*, you have to use plural adjective forms. For describing women, you simply use the regular feminine plural ending ـات **-aat** that you learned back in Lesson 2. Remember that the plural of مُدَرِّسة **mudarrisa** (*female teacher*) is مُدَرِّسات **mudarrisaat** (*female teachers*). The same ending goes on adjectives describing female humans.

نَحْنُ سَعيدات.	naHnu saxiidaat.	*We (f.) are happy.*
أَنْتُنَّ طَويلات.	'antunna Tawiilaat.	*You (f. pl.) are tall.*
هُنَّ تَعيسات.	hunna taxiisaat.	*They (f.) are sad.*

For describing human male plurals, though, things are a bit trickier. Remember from Lesson 2 that most Arabic nouns have so-called "broken" plurals. The three root consonants are kept in the same order, but vowels are added or deleted before, after, or in between those consonants. So, وَلَد **walad** (*boy*) becomes أَوْلاد **'awlaad** (*boys*), and بِنْت **bint** (*girl*) becomes بَنات **banaat** (*girls*).

Adjectives have broken plural forms as well, but they're only used to describe human males or groups of males and females. Just as with nouns, you have to memorize the broken plural forms of adjectives. The broken plural form of سَعيد **saxiid** (*happy*) is سُعَداء **suxadaa'**, and the broken plural form of طَويل **Tawiil** (*tall*) is طِوال **Tiwaal**.

هُم سُعَداء.	**hum suxadaa'.**	*They are happy. (m. or mixed)*
نَحْنُ سُعَداء.	**naHnu suxadaa'.**	*We are happy. (m. or mixed)*
أَنْتُم طِوال.	**'antum Tiwaal.**	*You are tall. (pl., m. or mixed)*

Take It Further: Arabic Script

Turn now to your script guide to cover another group of Arabic letters. Go to Part 1: Reading Arabic, and read:

- Group 6: س **s** and ش **sh**

Vocabulary Builder 2

Track: Lesson 5 Vocabulary Builder 2 (Track 3) CD: 2

pen	قَلَم	qalam
paper	وَرَقة	waraqa
book	كِتاب	kitaab
dress	فُسْتان	fustaan
shirt	قَميص	qamiiS
shoes	حِذاء	Hidhaa'
color	لَوْن	lawn
white	أَبْيَض	'abyaD
black	أَسْوَد	'aswad
green	أَخْضَر	'akhDar
blue	أَزْرَق	'azraq
red	أَحْمَر	'aHmar
yellow	أَصْفَر	'aSfar
brown	بُنيّ	bunnii

Vocabulary Practice 2

First, match the English in Column A to the Arabic in Column B.

1. *paper* — a. كِتاب **kitaab**
2. *shirt* — b. قَلَم **qalam**
3. *book* — c. وَرَقة **waraqa**
4. *pen* — d. حِذاء **Hidhaa'**
5. *shoes* — e. فُسْتان **fustaan**
6. *dress* — f. قَميص **qamiiS**

ANSWER KEY

1. c; 2. f; 3. a; 4. b; 5. d; 6. e

Now find the terms related to colors.

'	*a*	*S*	*f*	*a*	*r*	*b*	*u*
D	*'*	*a*	*z*	*r*	*a*	*q*	*'*
s	*l*	*D*	*y*	*'*	*m*	*a*	*b*
'	*a*	*s*	*w*	*a*	*d*	*d*	*u*
l	*w*	*x*	*w*	*b*	*u*	*a*	*n*
a	*n*	*r*	*a*	*y*	*D*	*n*	*n*
'	*a*	*H*	*m*	*a*	*r*	*b*	*i*
'	*a*	*k*	*h*	*D*	*a*	*r*	*i*

Fill them in below next to the Arabic script, along with their English translations:

ARABIC	ENGLISH
1. أَصْفَر	
2. أَبْيَض	
3. أَسْوَد	
4. أَخْضَر	
5. أَزْرَق	
6. أَحْمَر	
7. بُنيّ	
8. لَوْن	

Grammar Builder 2

Track: Lesson 5 Grammar Builder 2 (Track 4) CD: 2

COLOR ADJECTIVES AND DEMONSTRATIVES

Just like any other adjectives, colors agree with the nouns they describe in gender, number, and definiteness. The forms you just learned are the masculine singular forms, but a lot of the feminine forms are irregular. But wait, there's good news. Take a look at this:

أَبْيَض/بَيْضاء	'abyaD/bayDaa'	*white (m./f.)*
أَسْوَد/سَوْداء	'aswad/sawdaa'	*black (m./f.)*
أَخْضَر/خَضْراء	'akhDar/khaDraa'	*green (m./f.)*
أَزْرَق/زَرْقاء	'azraq/zarqaa'	*blue (m./f.)*
أَحْمَر/حَمْراء	'aHmar/Hamraa'	*red (m./f.)*
أَصْفَر/صَفْراء	'aSfar/Safraa'	*yellow (m./f.)*

Do you notice anything about all the masculine forms and all the feminine forms? Think about the three root consonants. If you replace all the consonants in the masculine forms with C (meaning "consonant"), you have the exact same pattern: 'aCCaC. (Keep in mind that kh is one consonant in Arabic: خ.) The feminine forms all follow the same pattern, too: CaCCaa'. Colors are a nice and simple way to get used to noticing root consonants in Arabic, and seeing how they're manipulated, often in systematic patterns. Here are some examples:

قَلَم أَزْرَق	qalam 'azraq	*a blue pen*
القَلَم الأَزْرَق	al-qalam al-'azraq	*the blue pen*
وَرَقة زَرْقاء	waraqa zarqaa'	*blue paper*
الوَرَقة الزَرْقاء	al-waraqa az-zarqaa'	*the blue paper*

Now let's look at how to say *this* and *these* in Arabic. Demonstrative adjectives, as they are called, also agree in gender and number with the noun they refer to.

هَذا	haadhaa*	*this (m.)*
هَذِه	haadhihi*	*this (f.)*
هَؤلاء	haa'ulaa'i	*these (pl.)*

*Even though these words are spelled with a short a in Arabic, the first vowel is pronounced long: aa.

If you're identifying something in a sentence, as in "*this is ...*," just begin with the appropriate demonstrative.

هَذا قَلَم.	haadhaa qalam.	*This is a pen.*
هَذِهِ وَرَقة.	haadhihi waraqa.	*This is a paper.*

Remember that non-human plurals take feminine singular agreement. So, هَذِه haadhihi (*this*) is used with feminine singulars as well as plural objects and animals. هَؤلاء haa'ulaa'i (*these*) is only used with human plurals, of both genders.

هَذِه مَدارِس.	haadhihi madaaris.	*These are schools.*
هَذِه مَوائِد.	haadhihi mawaa'id.	*These are tables.*
هَؤلاء رِجال طِوال.	haa'ulaa'i rijaal Tiwaal.	*These are tall men.*
هؤلاء نِساء طَويلات.	haa'ulaa'i nisaa' Tawiilaat.	*These are tall women.*

If you want to form a phrase with *this* or *these*, as in "*this book/man/woman is ...,*" begin with the appropriate demonstrative, and link it to the noun with ال al- (*the*).

هَذا الكِتاب كَبير.	haadhaa l-kitaab kabiir.	*This book is big.*
هؤلاء الرِجال طِوال.	haa'ulaa'i l-rijaal Tiwaal.	*These men are tall.*

Notice that when the word before ال al- (*the*) ends with a vowel, the a- is dropped in pronunciation.

Work Out 1

Track: Lesson 5 Work Out 1 (Track 5) CD: 2

Listen to the audio to hear several examples of adjectives and demonstratives. Listen a few times, and then complete the following exercise. Fill in the blanks with the correct demonstrative, and circle the correct form of the adjective. Then translate the full sentences.

1. __________ قَلَم أَزْرَق / زَرْقاء.

__________ qalam 'azraq / zarqaa'.

2. __________ وَرَقة أَبْيَض / بَيْضاء.

__________ waraqa abyaD / bayDaa'.

3. __________ فُسْتان أَحْمَر / حَمْراء.

__________ fustaan 'aHmar / Hamraa'.

4. قَميص أَسْوَد / سَوْداء . ______________

______________ qamiiS 'aswad / sawdaa'.

5. الرِجال طَويل /طِوال. ______________

______________ ar-rijaal Tawiil / Tiwaal.

6. الكِتاب كَبير / كَبيرة. ______________

______________ al-kitaab kabiir / kabiira.

ANSWER KEY

1. haadhaa, 'azraq (*This is a blue pen.*) 2. haadhihi, bayDaa' (*This is a white paper.*) 3. haadhaa, 'aHmar (*This is a red dress.*) 4. haadhaa, 'aswad (*This is a black shirt.*) 5. haa'ulaa'i, Tiwaal (*These men are tall.*) 6. haadhaa, kabiir (*This book is big.*)

Bring It All Together

Track: Lesson 5 Bring It All Together (Track 6) CD: 2

Now let's bring it all together and add a little bit more vocabulary and structure.

أنا سَعيد جِداً.	'anaa saxiid jiddan!	*I am very happy!*
عائِلَتي هُنا في بَيْتي.	xaa'ilatii hunaa fii baytii.	*My family is here in my house.*
هَذا إبْن أخي سَمير.	haadhaa 'ibn 'akhii samiir.	*This is my brother's son Samir.*
سَمير طِفْل.	samiir Tifl.	*Samir is a child.*
سَمير يُريد أنْ يَرْسُم.	samiir yuriid 'an yarsum.	*Samir wants to draw.*

أبوهُ يُعطيهِ قَلَم و وَرَقة.	'abuuhu yuxTiihi qalam wa waraqa.	*His father gives him a pen and a paper.*
سَمير يَرْسُم بِنْت.	samiir yarsum bint.	*Samir draws a girl.*
البِنْت تَرْتَدي فُسْتان أَحْمَر.	al-bint tartadii fustaan 'aHmar.	*The girl is wearing a red dress.*
شَعْر البِنْت بُنيّ.	shaxr al-bint bunnii.	*The girl's hair is brown.*
هذِهِ أُخْتُهُ الصَغيرة سامية.	haadhihi 'ukhtuhu aS-Saghiira saamiya.	*It's his little sister Samia.*

Take It Further

Track: Lesson 5 Take It Further (Track 7) CD: 2

Let's go over some of the new vocabulary that you just learned.

جِداً	jiddan	*very*
هُنا	hunaa	*here*
يُريد	yuriid	*(he) wants*
يَرسُم	yarsum	*(he) draws*
تَرْتَدي	tartadii	*(she) wears*
طِفْل	Tifl	*child, (m.)*
طِفْلَة	Tifla	*child, (f.)*

Now take a closer look at these two sentences:

سَمير يَرْسُم بِنْت.	samiir yarsum bint.	*Samir draws a girl.*
سَمير يُريد أنْ يَرْسُم.	samiir yuriid 'an yarsum.	*Samir wants to draw.*

You know that the verb يَرسُم yarsum means *(he) draws*, as in the first example above. But take a look at the second sentence, which contains the particle أنْ 'an. Arabic doesn't have an infinitive form (*to draw, to do, to go*, etc.), so the way you go about saying *wants to do* something is to use the verb يُريد yuriid (*he wants*), plus the particle أنْ 'an, plus another conjugated verb, for example يَرْسُم yarsum (*he draws*.) You get something like: *he wants that he should draw*, meaning simply *he wants to draw*.

That second verb is technically in a special form of the present tense called the subjunctive, but you'll learn more about that in your advanced studies of Arabic. In any event, it often sounds just like the regular old present tense in spoken Arabic, so don't worry too much about it.

Work Out 2

First, choose the correct form of the adjectives in each of the phrases or sentences below, and translate your answers.

1. (طَويل / طَويلَة / طِوال / طَويلات) ______________ رِجال
rijaal ______________ (Tawiil / Tawiila / Tiwaal / Tawiilaat)

2. (سَعيد / سَعيدة / سُعَداء / سَعيدات) ______________ هُنَّ
hunna ______________ (saxiid / saxiida / suxadaa' / saxiidaat)

3. (صَغير / صَغيرة / الصِغار / الصَغيرة) ______________ البِنْت
al-bint ______________ (Saghiir / Saghiira / aS-Saghiir / aS-Saghiira)

4. (سَعيدة / سَعيد / سُعَداء / سَعيدات) ______________ الوَلَد
al-walad ______________ (saxiida / saxiid / suxadaa' / saxiidaat)

5. (أَحْمَر / حَمْراء) ______________ الكِتاب
al-kitaab ______________ ('aHmar / Hamraa')

6. (طَويل / طَويلات / طِوال / طَويلة) ______________ هيَ
hiya ______________ (Tawiil / Tawiilaat / Tiwaal / Tawiila)

7. (سَعيد / سُعَداء / سَعيدة / سَعيدات) ______________ أنْتِ
'anti ______________ (saxiid / suxadaa' / saxiida / saxiidaat)

8. (أَزْرَق / زَرْقاء) ______________ الوَرَقة
al-waraqa ______________ ('azraq / zarqaa')

9. (طَويلات / طِوال / طَويلة / طَويل) ______________ هَؤلاء نِساء
haa'ulaa' nisaa' ______________ (Tawiilaat / Tiwaal / Tawiila / Tawiil)

10. (صَغيرات / صَغيرة / صِغار / صَغير) ______________ الطِفلة
aT-Tifla ______________ (Saghiiraat / Saghiira / Sighaar / Saghiir)

ANSWER KEY

1. rijaal Tiwaal (*tall men*) 2. hunna saxiidaat (*They (f.) are happy.*) 3. al-bint aS-Saghiira (*the little girl*) or: al-bint-Saghiira (*the girl is little*) 4. al-walad saxiid (*the boy is happy*) 5. al-kitaab 'aHmar (*the book is red*) 6. hiya Tawiila (*she is tall*) 7. 'anti saxiida (*you (f.) are happy*) 8. al-waraqa zarqaa' (*the paper is blue*) 9. haa'ulaa' nisaa' Tawiilaat (*These are tall women*) 10. aT-Tifla Saghiira (*the child (f.) is small*).

Drive It Home

This lesson covered a lot of information that you need to know in order to describe things, namely adjective agreement. Let's take a moment to do some careful review to help you remember the important patterns. Use each adjective below, in the appropriate form, to describe the noun that follows it, and translate your answers.

1. كبير kabiir: وَلَد walad, بَيْت bayt, رَجُل rajul, كِتاب kitaab, قَلَم qalam

2. صَغير Saghiir: الوَلَد al-walad, البَيْت al-bayt, الرَجُل ar-rajul, الكِتاب al-kitaab, الفُسْتان al-fustaan

3. طَويل Tawiil: البِنْت al-bint, الإمْرأة al-'imra'a, الأُخْت al-'ukht, المائِدة al-maa'ida المُدَرِّسة al-mudarrisa

4. سَعيد saxiid: البَنات al-banaat, النِساء an-nisaa', الأخَوات al-'akhawaat, المُدَرِّسات al-mudarrisaat

5. أَزْرَق 'azraq: الكِتاب al-kitaab, القَلَم al-qalam, القَميص al-qamiiS, الفُسْتان al-fustaan, البَيْت al-bayt

---

6. سَعيد saxiid: أَولاد 'awlaad, رِجال rijaal, مُدَرِّسون mudarrisuun, أَزْواج 'azwaaj, آباء 'aabaa'

ANSWER KEY

1. walad kabiir (*a big boy*), bayt kabiir (*a big house*), rajul kabiir (*a big/old man*), kitaab kabiir (*a big book*), qalam kabiir (*a big pen*)
2. al-walad aS-Saghiir (*the small boy*), al-bayt aS-Saghiir (*the small house*), ar-rajul aS-Saghiir (*the small/young man*), al-kitaab aS-Saghiir (*the small book*), al-fustaan aS-Saghiir (*the small dress*).
3. al-bint aT-Tawiila (*the tall girl*), al-'imra'a T-Tawiila (*the tall woman*), al-'ukht aT-Tawiila (*the tall sister*), al-maa'ida T-Tawiila (*the long table*), al-mudarrisa T-Tawiila (*the tall teacher*)
4. al-banaat as-saxiidaat (*the happy girls*), al-'akhawaat as-saxiidaat (*the happy sisters*), al-mudarrisaat as-saxiidaat (*the happy teachers*)
5. al-kitaab al-'azraq (*the blue book*), al-qalam al-'azraq (*the blue pen*), al-qamiiS al-'azraq (*the blue shirt*), al-fustaan al-'azraq (*the blue dress*), al-bayt al-'azraq (*the blue house*)
6. 'awlaad suxadaa' (*happy boys*), rijaal suxadaa' (*happy men*), mudarrisuun suxadaa' (*happy teachers (m.)*), 'azwaaj suxadaa' (*happy husbands*), 'aabaa' suxadaa' (*happy fathers*)

Take It Further: Arabic Script

Turn now back to your script guide to learn how to write the letters you learned earlier in this lesson. Go to Part 2: Writing Arabic, and do:

- Group 6: س and ش

Parting Words

In this lesson, you learned how to describe things with some basic vocabulary and structures for talking about your surroundings. Here's what you did:

- ☐ Reviewed pronouns, and learned a few new ones (Still unsure? Go back to 100.)
- ☐ Learned how to use them with some more basic descriptive terms (Still unsure? Go back to 102.)
- ☐ Learned the words for everyday objects and colors (Still unsure? Go back to 105.)
- ☐ Used words like *this* and *these* (Still unsure? Go back to 107.)

Put it all to use in sentences that bring together a lot of what you've been learning (Still unsure? Go back to 111.)

Don't forget to practice and reinforce what you've learned by visiting **www.livinglanguage.com/languagelab** for flashcards, games, and quizzes.

Word Recall

Let's review some of the vocabulary you've learned so far. Translate the following into English.

1. مَساء الخَيْر masaa' al-khayr ______
2. ما إسْمُك؟ maa 'ismuk? ______
3. نَعَم naxam ______
4. إلى اللِقاء 'ilaa l-liqaa' ______
5. عائلة كبيرة xaa'ila kabiira ______
6. أنا دكتور. 'anaa duktuur. ______
7. سَبعة نِساء sabxat nisaa' ______
8. مَطْبَخ maTbakh ______
9. يَكْتُب yaktub ______
10. مَدْرَسَتُهُم madrasatuhum ______
11. أَنْتُم طِوال. 'antum Tiwaal. ______
12. القَلَم الأَزْرَق al-qalam al-'azraq ______
13. أنا سَعيد 'anaa saxiid. ______
14. هَذِهِ طِفلة. haadhihi Tifla. ______
15. غُرْفة النَوْم ghurfat an-nawm ______

ANSWER KEY:

1. *Good evening.* 2. *What's your name?* 3. *yes;* 4. *see you later/good bye;* 5. *a big family;* 6. *I am a doctor.* 7. *seven women;* 8. *a kitchen;* 9. *He writes.* 10. *their school;* 11. *You (pl.) are tall.* 12. *the blue pen;* 13. *I am happy.* 14. *This is a child (f.).* 15. *the bedroom*

Quiz 1

الإمتحان الأوَّل

al-'imtiHaan al-'awwal

You've made it halfway through the course! Congratulations! Now let's see how you've done so far. In this section you'll find a short quiz testing what you learned in Lessons 1–5. After you've answered all of the questions, score your quiz and see how you did. If you find that you need to go back and review, please do so before continuing on to Lesson 6.

You'll get a second quiz after Lesson 10, followed by a final review with five dialogues and comprehension questions. Let's get started!

A. Match the following English words to the correct Arabic translations:

1. رَجُل rajul	a. *woman*
2. إمرأة 'imra'a	b. *family*
3. زَوجة zawja	c. *man*
4. عائِلة xaa'ila	d. *son*
5. إبن 'ibn	e. *wife*

B. Translate the following English expressions into Arabic:

1. *What's your (m.) name?* ________________

2. *Good bye.* ________________

3. *How are you?* ________________

4. *Where are you (f.) from?* ________________

5. *Good morning.* ________________

C. Fill in the missing forms of each noun.

SINGULAR	DUAL	PLURAL
وَلَد **walad**	وَلَدان **waladaan**	*1.* ________
بِنت **bint**	*2.* ________	بنات **banaat**
3. ________	عائلتان **xaa'ilataan**	عائلات **xaa'ilaat**
مُدَرِّس **mudarris**	مُدَرِّسان **mudarrisaan**	*4.* ________
مُدَرِّسة **mudarrisa**	*5.* ________	مُدَرِّسات **mudarrisaat**

D. Fill in the table with the correct forms of يأكُل **ya'kul** (*eat*):

I eat	*1.*
you (m.) eat	*2.*
you (f.) eat	*3.*

he eats	4.
she eats	5.
we eat	6.
you (m. pl.) eat	7.
the two of you eat	8.
they (m.) eat	9.
the men eat	10.

ANSWER KEY

A. 1. c; 2. a; 3. e; 4. b; 5. d

B. 1. ما إسمُكَ؟ maa 'ismuka; 2. مَعَ السلامة maxa s-salaama; 3. كيف الحال؟ kayf al-Haal?; 4. مِن أين أنت؟ min 'ayna 'anta?; 5. صَباح الخَيْر. SabaaH al-khayr

C. 1. أولاد 'awlaad; 2. بِنتان bintaan; 3. عائلة xaa'ila; 4. مُدَرِّسون mudarrisuun; 5. مُدَرِّستان mudarrisataan

D. 1. آكُل 'aakul; 2. تأكُل ta'kul; 3. تأكُلين ta'kuliin; 4. يأكُل ya'kul; 5. تأكُل ta'kul; 6. نأكُل na'kul; 7. تأكُلون ta'kuluun; 8. تأكُلان ta'kulaan; 9. يأكُلون ya'kuluun; 10. الرِجال يأكُلون ar-rijaal ya'kuluun

How Did You Do?

Give yourself a point for every correct answer, then use the following key to determine whether or not you're ready to move on:

0–10 points: It's probably best to go back and study the lessons again to make sure you understood everything completely. Take your time; it's not a race! Make sure you spend time reviewing the vocabulary and reading through each Grammar Builder section carefully.

11–18 points: If the questions you missed were in sections A or B, you may want to review the vocabulary from previous lessons again; if you missed answers mostly in sections C or D, check the Grammar Builder sections to make sure you have your grammar basics down.

19–25 points: Feel free to move on to Lesson 6! You're doing a great job.

| | | points

Lesson 6: Around Town

الدَرْس السادِس: في المدينة

ad-dars as-saadis: fi l-madiina

كيف الحال؟ kayf al-Haal? *How are you?* Ready for lesson 6? This lesson will take you from Point A to Point B in a town, so you'll learn how to:

- ☐ Use basic vocabulary for getting around town
- ☐ Ask questions so you won't get lost
- ☐ Use basic direction phrases
- ☐ Express location
- ☐ Put it all to use in a short dialogue about asking directions

Let's start with some basic vocabulary.

Vocabulary Builder 1

Track: Lesson 6 Vocabulary Builder 1 (Track 8) CD: 2

post office	مَكْتَب البَريد	maktab al-bariid
pharmacy	صَيدَليَّة	Saydaliyya
hospital	مُستَشفى	mustashfaa
supermarket	بِقالة	biqaala

university	جامِعة	jaamixa
airport	مَطار	maTaar
hotel	فُنْدُق	funduq
taxi	سيّارة أُجرة	sayyaarat 'ujra
address	عُنوان	xunwaan
street	شارِع	shaarix
square	مَيدان	maydaan
intersection	تقاطُع	taqaaTux

Vocabulary Practice 1

Let's try a little bit of script practice with your new vocabulary. Can you match the Arabic Script with the meaning in English? The transliteration is given in the answer key to help you check how your reading is coming along!

1. *hotel*	a. جامِعة
2. *address*	b. شارِع
3. *supermarket*	c. عُنوان
4. *street*	d. فُنْدُق
5. *airport*	e. بِقالة
6. *university*	f. مَطار

ANSWER KEY:

1. d, funduq, 2. c, xunwaan, 3. e, biqaala, 4. b, shaarix, 5. f, maTaar, 6. a, jaamixa

Grammar Builder 1

Track: Lesson 6 Grammar Builder 1 (Track 9) CD: 2

ASKING QUESTIONS

Now let's talk a bit about asking questions in Arabic. To ask a yes-no question, one with the answer either نَعَم naxam or لا laa, use the particle هَل hal at the beginning of the question.

هل هذه صَيدَليّة؟	hal haadhihi Saydaliyya?	*Is this a pharmacy?*
هَل شارِع النُزهة قَريب مِن هُنا؟	hal shaarix an-nuzha qariib min hunaa?	*Is Al-Nozha Street near here?*

Of course you can also ask questions with question words. You've already seen the question word ما maa (*what*), which is only used with the (understood) verb *be*. Here are some other common question words.

ما؟	maa?	*What? (with be questions)*
ما هذا؟	maa haadhaa?	*What is this?*
ماذا؟	maadhaa?	*What? (with other verbs)*
ماذا تَعْمَل؟	maadhaa taxmal?	*What do you do?*
أيْنَ؟	'ayna?	*Where?*

أيْن الْجامِعَة؟	'ayn al-jaamixa?	*Where is the university?*
مِنْ أيْن؟	min 'ayn?	*From where?*
مِنْ أيْن لوسي؟	min 'ayn luusii?	*Where is Lucy from?*
مَن؟	man?	*Who?*
مَن لوسي؟	man luusii?	*Who is Lucy?*
مَتى؟	mataa?	*When?*
مَتى تعمَل؟	mataa taxmal?	*When do you work?*
كَيْفَ؟	kayfa?	*How?*
كَيْف الحال؟	kayf al-Haal?	*How are you?*

Note that you will hear both 'ayn and 'ayna (*where*) and kayfa and kayfa (*how*).

Take It Further: Arabic Script

Turn to your script guide to cover yet another group of Arabic letters. This time you'll take a look at the "emphatic" consonants, so go to Part 1: Reading Arabic, and read:

- ☐ Group 7: ص S, ض D, ط T, and ظ DH

Vocabulary Builder 2

Track: Lesson 6 Vocabulary Builder 2 (Track 10) CD: 2

here	هُنا	hunaa
there	هُناك	hunaak
near	قَريب	qariib
far	بَعيد	baxiid
right	يَمين	yamiin
left	يَسار	yasaar
before	قَبْل	qabl
after	بَعْد	baxd
in front of	أمام	'amaam
behind	خَلْف	khalf
next to	بِجانِب	bijaanib
straight ahead	إلى الأمام	'ilaa l-'amaam

Vocabulary Practice 2

Translate the following into Arabic.

1. *next to* __________
2. *behind* __________
3. *near* __________

4. *far* ____________________

5. *left* ____________________

6. *right* ____________________

7. *there* ____________________

8. *here* ____________________

ANSWERS:

1. بِجانِب bijaanib; 2. خَلْف khalf; 3. قَريب qariib; 4. بَعيد baxiid; 5. يَسار yasaar; 6. يَمين yamiin; 7. هُناك hunaak; 8. هُنا hunaa

Grammar Builder 2

Track: Lesson 6 Grammar Builder 2 (Track 11) CD: 2

EXPRESSING LOCATION

Let's go over these new words one more time. You've heard several prepositions and words that will help you describe the placement of things around you.

هُنا	hunaa	*here*
هُناك	hunaak	*there*
قَريب	qariib	*near*
بَعيد	baxiid	*far*
يَمين	yamiin	*right*
يَسار	yasaar	*left*
قَبل	qabl	*before*

بَعد	baxd	*after*
أَمام	'amaam	*in front of*
خَلْف	khalf	*behind*
بِجانِب	bijaanib	*next to*
إلى الأمام	'ilaa l-'amaam	*straight ahead*

To ask for directions, you will also need the question word أَيْنَ 'ayn? (*where?*). A lot of Arabic location expressions are held together by various prepositions; for example, the preposition مِن min (*from*) is used together with the adjective قَريب qariib (*near*) to say قَريب مِن qariib min (*close to*). Another word for *from* is عَن xan, used in conjunction with the adjective بَعيد baxiid (*far*) in the phrase بَعيد عَن baxiid xan (*far from*). You might also have spotted the preposition إلى 'ilaa (*to* or *towards*), which you heard used in the expression إلى الأَمام 'ilaa l-'amaam, meaning *towards the front* or *straight ahead*.

Work Out 1

Track: Lesson 6 Work Out 1 (Track 12) CD: 2

First, listen to the audio, which includes some questions and answers related to asking directions and getting around town. You'll hear a lot of vocabulary and constructions you've learned in this lesson. Familiarize yourself with the sentences by listening to them a few times, and by repeating what you hear. Then, fill in the blanks in each sentence below with the missing word or phrase.

1. *Where is this street?*

   هذا الشارِع؟ ________________

   ________________ haadhaa sh-shaarix?

2. *The supermarket is near the hotel.*

   البِقالة قَريبة مِن ________________.

   al-biqaala qariiba min ________________.

3. *The pharmacy is behind the post office.*

   الصَيدَلية خَلف ________________.

   aS-Saydaliyya khalf ________________.

4. *Is the taxi here?*

   ________________ سَيّارة الأُجْرة ________________.

   ________________ sayyarrat al-'ujra ________________?

5. *There is an intersection before the square.*

   ________________ تقاطُع ________________ المَيْدان.

   ________________ taqaaTux ________________ al-maydaan.

6. *Is this address far?*

   هَل هذا الـ________________.

   hal haadha al-________________?

7. *The hospital is behind the university.*

   ________________ خَلْف ________________.

   ________________ khalf ________________.

8. *I am in front of the post office.*

مَكْتَب البَريد. ______________

______________ maktab al-bariid.

ANSWER KEY

1. أَيْنَ 'ayna; 2. الفُنْدُق al-funduq; 3. مَكْتَب البَريد maktab al-bariid; 4. هَل hal, هُنا hunaa; 5. هُناك hunaaka, قَبل qabl; 6.عُنوان xunwaan, بَعيد baxiid; 7. المُستَشفى al-mustashfaa, الجامِعة al-jaamixa; 8. انا 'anaa, أَمام 'amaam

Bring It All Together

Track: Lesson 6 Bring It All Together (Track 13) CD: 2

Now let's bring it all together, and add a little bit more vocabulary and structure.

عفواً ، أبحَثُ عَن هذا العُنوان.	xafwan, 'abHathu xan haadhaa l-xunwaan.	*Excuse me, I am looking for this address.*
هذا الفُنْدُق في شارِع النُزْهة.	haadhaa l-funduq fii shaarix an-nuzha.	*This hotel is on Al-Nozha Street.*
هَل شارِع النُزهة قَريب مِن هُنا؟	hal shaarix an-nuzha qariib min hunaa?	*Is Al-Nozha Street near here?*
نَعَم ، شارِع النُزْهة خَلْف مَيْدان الثَورة.	naxam, shaarix an-nuzha khalf maydaan ath-thawra.	*Yes, Al-Nozha street is behind Al-Thawra Square.*
وَأيْنَ هذا المَيدان؟	wa 'ayna haadhaa l-maydaan?	*And where is this square?*

هذا المَيْدان بَعْد التقاطُع وَقبلَ الجامِعة الأمريكية.	haadhaa l-maydaan baxd at-taqaaTux wa qabl al-jaamiixa al-amriikiiyya.	*This square is after the intersection and before the American University.*
الفُندُق إلى يَسار صَيْدليّة الصِحّة وَبِجانِب مَكْتَب البَريد.	al-funduq 'ilaa yasaar Saydaliyyat aS-SiHHa wa bijaanib maktab al-bariid.	*The hotel is to the left of the Sihha pharmacy and next to the post office.*
هَل أَحْتاج إلى سيّارة أُجْرة؟	hal 'aHtaaj 'ilaa sayyarat 'ujra?	*Do I need a taxi?*
كلا ، إنّه قريب من هُنا.	kallaa, 'innahu qariib min hunaa.	*No, it's close to here.*
وَإنّها نُزْهة جَميلة.	wa 'innahaa nuzha jamiila.	*and it's a nice walk.*
شُكراً لِمُساعَدَتِكَ.	shukran li-musaaxadatika.	*Thank you for your help.*

Take It Further

Track: Lesson 6 Take It Further (Track 14) CD: 2

Let's take a moment to review some of what you heard in Bring It All Together. You saw several examples of هذا haadhaa (*this*) followed by a noun introduced by ال al- (*the*). Remember that the article is used to link the noun in a *this*-phrase. Notice that the fatHa, or short a, in ال al- is dropped in pronunciation when the word before it ends in a vowel, as in the case of هذا haadhaa (*this*).

هذا العُنوان	haadhaa l-xunwaan	*this address*
هذا الفُنْدُق	haadhaa l-funduq	*this hotel*
هذا المَيْدان	haadhaa l-maydaan	*this square*

You were also introduced to another verb, أَبْحَثُ 'abHathu (*I look for*). It takes a lot of practice to master verb conjugation, so let's take this opportunity to go over the important forms. Let's start with the singular and plural forms. We'll add the forms for two new pronouns that you learned in the previous lesson أَنْتُنَّ 'antunna (*you, f., pl.*) and هُنَّ hunna (*they, f.*) We'll also use the suffix -u, which you'll sometimes hear, especially in more formal settings, as well as the suffix -a on the *you*, f., *you*, pl., and *they* forms.

PRONOUN	PREFIX	SUFFIX	LOOK FOR
'anaa (*I*) أنا	'a- أَ	-u ُ	'abHathu أَبْحَثُ
'anta (*you, m.*) أَنْتَ	ta- تَـ	-u ُ	tabHathu تَبحَثُ
'anti (*you, f.*) أَنْتِ	ta- تَـ	-iina ينَ	tabHathiina تَبْحَثينَ
huwa (*he*) هوَ	ya- يَـ	-u ُ	yabHathu يَبْحَثُ
hiya (*she*) هيَ	ta- تَـ	-u ُ	tabHathu تَبْحَثُ

PRONOUN	PREFIX	SUFFIX	LOOK FOR
naHnu (*we*) نَحنُ	na- نَـ	-u ُ	nabHathu نَبْحَثُ
'antum (*you, pl.*) أَنْتُم	ta- تَـ	-uuna ونَ	tabHathuuna تَبْحَثونَ
'antunna (*you, f., pl.*) أَنْتُنَّ	ta- تَـ	-na نَ	tabHathna تَبْحَثْنَ
hum (*they, m.*) هُم	ya- يَـ	-uuna ونَ	yabHathuuna يَبْحَثونَ
hunna (*they, f.*) هُنَّ	ya- يَـ	-na نَ	yabHathna يَبْحَثْنَ

Let's break all of that down so that it's easier to digest and remember. Here are a few simple bullet points to remember that will make it much easier to use Arabic verbs.

PREFIXES:

- ☐ All of the *you* forms, whether singular or plural, masculine or feminine, have the prefix تَـ ta-.
- ☐ All of the third person forms (not *I*, *you*, or *we*) have the prefix يَـ ya-, with one exception: هيَ hiya (*she*) has the prefix تَـ ta-.

- The prefixes for أنا 'anaa (*I*) and نَحْنُ naHnu (*we*) are easy enough to remember, because they begin with the same two letters of the pronouns: أَ 'a- and نَـ na- respectively.

SUFFIXES:

- Almost all of the singular suffixes, as well as the one for نَحْنُ naHnu (*we*), are ُ -u. Remember that this is often dropped in speech. Feminine أَنْتِ 'anti (*you*) has the suffix ينَ -iina.
- For the plural forms of *you*, and the forms of *they*, the masculine suffix is ونَ -uuna and the feminine suffix is نَ -na.

Now let's add the dual forms. There's one pronoun for the *two of you*, and one verb form. Again, since it's a *you* form, it takes the prefix تَـ ta-. There's also just one pronoun for dual *they*, but the verb forms are different depending on whether you're talking about two males or two females. But in all cases, the dual suffix is انِ -aani.

'antumaa (*the two of you, m. or f.*) أنتُما	ta- تَـ	-aani انِ	tabHathaani تَبْحَثانِ
humaa (*the two of them, m.*) هُما	ya- يَـ	-aani انِ	yabHathaani يَبْحَثانِ

humaa (*the two of them, f.*) هُما	ta- تَـ	-aani انِ	tabHathaani تَبْحَثانِ

And now, you've reviewed all of the personal pronouns and all of the present tense verb forms in Arabic! مَبْروك mabruuk! *Congratulations!*

Work Out 2

Let's practice asking where things are. Use أيْنَ 'ayna ... (*where is ...*) with the following words, then translate your answers.

1. مَكْتَب البَريد maktab al-bariid ____________________
2. المُسْتَشْفى al-mustashfaa ____________________
3. البِقالة al-biqaala ____________________
4. هذا العُنوان haadha l-xunwaan ____________________
5. الجامِعة al-jaamixa ____________________
6. المَطار al-maTaar ____________________
7. صَيْدَليّة كَبيرة Saydaliyya kabiira ____________________
8. الفُندُق الجَديد al-funduq al-jadiid ____________________

ANSWER KEY

1. 'ayna maktab al-bariid? (*Where is the post office?*) 2. 'ayna l-mustashfaa? (*Where is the hospital?*) 3. 'ayna l-biqaala? (*Where is the supermarket?*) 4. 'ayna haadha l-xunwaan? (*Where is this address?*) 5. 'ayna l-jaamixa? (*Where is the university?*) 6. 'ayna l-maTaar? (*Where is the airport?*) 7. 'ayna Saydaliyya kabiira? (*Where is a big pharmacy?*) 8. 'ayna l-funduq l-jadiid? (*Where is the new hotel?*)

Now, give the opposite of each of the following direction or location terms. Translate each pair of words:

1. بَعيد baxiid ≠ ________________
2. هُناكَ hunaaka ≠ ________________
3. يَسار yasaar ≠ ________________
4. قَبْل qabl ≠ ________________
5. خَلْف khalf ≠ ________________

ANSWER KEY

1. قَريب qariib (*near ≠ far*); 2. هُنا hunaa (*there ≠ here*); 3. يَمين yamiin (*left ≠ right*); 4. بَعد baxd (*before ≠ after*); 5. أَمام 'amaam (*behind ≠ in front of*)

Drive It Home

Let's practice using هذا haadhaa (*this, m.*) and هذِه haadhihi (*this, f.*) in phrases such as *this pharmacy*. Remember that you have to connect the form of *this* to the noun with the definite article الـ al-. First, let's try some masculine nouns. Translate your answers. Don't forget that the a in al- is dropped when the word before it ends in a vowel, and remember the pronunciation changes of the l in al-, too!

1. مَطار maTaar ______________________

2. فُنْدُق funduq ______________________

3. عُنوان xunwaan ______________________

4. مَيْدان maydaan ______________________

5. بَيْت bayt ______________________

6. رَجُل rajul ______________________

ANSWER KEY

1. haadhaa l-maTaar (*this airport*); 2. haadhaa l-funduq (*this hotel*); 3. haadhaa l-xunwaan (*this address*); 4. haadhaa l-maydaan (*this square*); 5. haadhaa l-bayt (*this house*); 6. haadhaa r-rajul (*this man*).

Great. Now, let's try some feminine nouns.

1. صَيْدَلِيّة Saydaliyya ______________________

2. مُسْتَشفى mustashfaa ______________________

3. بِقالة biqaala ______________________

4. جامِعة jaamixa ______________________

ANSWER KEY

1. haadhihi S-Saydaliyya (*this pharmacy*); 2. haadhihi l-mustashfaa (*this hospital*); 3. haadhihi l-biqaala (*this supermarket*); 4. haadhihi l-jaamixa (*this university*).

Now let's practice some *yes* questions. Answer each question with نَعَم naxam, following the example written below. Then translate both question and answer.

هَل هذا الفُندُق جَديد؟ hal haadhaa l-funduq jadiid?
نَعَم، هذا الفُنْدُق جَديد. naxam, haadhaa l-funduq jadiid.
Is this hotel new? Yes, this hotel is new.

1. هَل هذا العُنوان قَريب؟ hal haadhaa l-xunwaan qariib?

2. هَل هذه الجامِعة كَبيرة؟ hal haadhihi l-jaamixa kabiira?

3. هَل هذِه المُستشفى بَعيدة؟ hal haadhihi l-mustashfaa baxiida?

4. هَل هذا البَيْت صَغير؟ hal haadhaa l-bayt Saghiir?

5. هَل هذا المَطار كَبير؟ hal haadhaa l-maTaar kabiir?

6. هَل هذه الصَدَليّة قَريبة؟ hal haadhihi S-Saydaliyya qariiba?

7. هَل هذا الشارِع مُشْمِس؟ hal haadhaa sh-shaarix mushmis?

8. هَل هذا المَيدان أَمام الفُنْدُق؟ hal haadhaa l-maydaan 'amaam al-funduq?

ANSWER KEY

1. naxam, haadhaa l-xunwaan qariib. *(Is this address nearby? Yes, this address is nearby.)* 2. naxam, haadhihi l-jaamixa kabiira. *(Is this university big? Yes, this university is big.)* 3. naxam, haadhihi l-mustashfaa baxiida. *(Is this hospital far? Yes, this hospital is far.)* 4. naxam, haadhaa l-bayt Saghiir. *(Is this house small? Yes, this house is small.)* 5. naxam, haadhaa l-maTaar kabiir. *(Is this airport big? Yes, this airport is big.)* 6. naxam, haadhihi S-Saydaliyya qariiba. *(Is this pharmacy nearby? Yes, this pharmacy is nearby.)* 7. naxam, haadhaa sh-shaarix mushmis. *(Is this street sunny? Yes, this street is sunny.)* 8. naxam, haadhaa l-maydaan 'amaam al-funduq. *(Is this square in front of the hotel? Yes, this square is in front of the hotel.)*

Take It Further: Arabic Script

Turn back to your script guide to practice writing the letters you learned earlier in the lesson. Go to Part 2: Writing Arabic, and complete:

- Group 7: ص, ض, ط, and ظ

Parting Words

In this lesson, you learned a lot of new vocabulary, and you practiced more important basic constructions. You should know how to:

- ☐ Use basic vocabulary for getting around town (Still unsure? Go back to 123.)
- ☐ Ask questions so you won't get lost (Still unsure? Go back to 125.)
- ☐ Use basic direction phrases (Still unsure? Go back to 127.)
- ☐ Express location (Still unsure? Go back to 128.)

□ Put it all to use in a short dialogue about asking directions (Still unsure? Go back to 131.)

Don't forget to practice and reinforce what you've learned by visiting **www.livinglanguage.com/languagelab** for flashcards, games, and quizzes.

Take It Further

Track: Lesson 6 Take It Further (Track 15) CD: 2

You'll notice that a lot of English and French words have been borrowed into colloquial dialects of Arabic.

سوبِر ماركِت	suubermarkit	*supermarket*
تكسي	taksii	*taxi*
مَصْرَف ، بَنْك	maSraf, bank	*bank*
سينَما	siinama	*movies, cinema*

Word Recall

Let's do a cumulative review of the most important vocabulary you have learned in Lessons 3 through 6. Use the words from the word bank to complete the sentences below, then translate your answers into English.

a. قَريب qariib; b. بَيْت bayt; c. تَنام tanaam; d. الرَجُل ar-rajul; e. طالِبة Taaliba; f. يَجْلِس yajlis; g. أهْلاً 'ahlan; h. خَمَس khamas

1. إسْمي مُحَمَّد. __________

__________ 'ismii muHammad.

2. هِيَ __________ في المَدْرَسة.

hiya __________ fi l-madrasa.

3. __________ سَعيد.

__________ saxiid.

4. أَسْكُن في __________ كَبير.

'askun fii __________ kabiir.

5. أَحْمَد في غُرْفة المَكْتَب. __________

__________ 'ahmad fii ghurfat al-maktab.

6. بَيْتي __________ مِن المَدْرَسة.

baytii __________ min al-madrasa.

7. أسكُنُ مَعَ __________ نِساء.

'askun maxa __________ nisaa'.

8. مُنى __________ في سرير.

munaa __________ fii sariir.

ANSWER KEY

1. g, *Hello, My name is Mohammed.* 2. e, *She is a student at school.* 3. d, *The man in happy.* 4. b, *I live in a big house.* 5. f, *Ahmad sits in the study/office.* 6. a, *My house is close to the school.* 7. h, *I live with five women.* 8. c *Mona sleeps in a bed.*

Now, match the English phrases and sentences with the Arabic equivalents.

1. This hotel is new	a. هَل المَطار قَريب؟ hal al-maTaar qariib?
2. What is this?	b. مَكْتَب البَريد بِجانِب البِقالة. maktab al-bariid bijaanib al-biqaala.
3. The pharmacy is in front of the university.	c. هذا العُنوان بَعيد. haadhaa l-xunwaan baxiid.
4. Where is the hospital?	d. أَحْتاج إلى سَيّارة أُجْرة. 'aHtaaju 'ilaa sayyaarat 'ujra.
5. This address is far.	e. ما هذا؟ maa haadhaa?
6. The post office is next to the supermarket.	f. هذا الفندق جديد. haadhaa l-funduq jadiid.
7. I need a taxi.	g. أينَ المُسْتَشفى؟ 'ayna l-mustashfaa?
8. Is the airport close/near?	h. الصَيْدَليّة أمام الجامِعة. aS-Saydaliyya 'amaam al-jaamixa.

ANSWER KEY:

1. f; 2. e, 3. h; 4. g; 5. c; 6. b; 7. d; 8. a

Lesson 7: At the Restaurant

الدرس السابِع: في المَطْعَم

ad-dars as-saabix: fi l-maTxam

مَرْحَباً **marHaban!** *Hello!* This lesson is all about food and restaurants, so you'll learn:

- □ Basic vocabulary for meals
- □ How to say the names of common food and drink items
- □ Important vocabulary for use in a restaurant
- □ Key phrases for ordering food
- □ How to put it all together in a dialogue about ordering a meal

First, here's some vocabulary to get you started. هيّا نَبْدَأ **hayyaa nabda'!** *Let's begin!*

Vocabulary Builder 1

Track: Lesson 7 Vocabulary Builder 1 (Track 16) CD: 2

please	مِن فَضْلَك	**min faDlak**
breakfast	فُطور	**fuTuur**
lunch	غَداء	**ghadaa'**

dinner	عَشاء	xashaa'
restaurant	مَطْعَم	maTxam
café	مَقهى	maqhaa
tea	شاي	shaay
coffee	قَهوَة	qahwa
milk	حَليب	Haliib
sugar	سُكَّر	sukkar
water	ماء	maa'
menu	قائمة الطَعام	qaa'imat aT-Taxaam

Vocabulary Practice 1

Match the English with the Arabic words:

1. *breakfast* a. مِن فَضْلَك min faDlak
2. *restaurant* b. قَهْوة qahwa
3. *coffee* c. حَليب Haliib
4. *milk* d. سُكَّر sukkar
5. *sugar* e. مَطْعَم maTxam
6. *please* f. فُطور fuTuur

ANSWERS KEY:

1. f; 2. e; 3. b; 4. c; 5. d; 6. a

Grammar Builder 1

Track: Lesson 7 Grammar Builder 1 (Track 17) CD: 2

TALKING ABOUT FOOD

Let's review the vocabulary you learned. First, the meals of the day are:

فطور	fuTuur	*breakfast*
غَداء	ghadaa'	*lunch*
عَشاء	xashaa'	*dinner*

The drinks you learned are:

شاي	shaay	*tea*
قَهوَة	qahwa	*coffee*
حَليب	Haliib	*milk*
ماء	maa'	*water*

If you're having شاي shaay (*tea*) or قَهوَة qahwa (*coffee*), you might ask for سُكَّر sukkar (*sugar*) or حَليب Haliib (*milk*). Two places where you might eat or drink are:

مَطْعَم	maTxam	*restaurant*
مَقهى	maqhaa	*café*

And two expressions that will come in handy in either are:

مِن فَضْلَك	min faDlak	*please*
قائمة الطَعام	qaa'imat aT-Taxaam	*menu*

Here are some verbs that you can use to talk about eating. Notice that the verb يَتَناوَل yatanaawal means *eat* as in *eat a meal*, so it can be used with الفُطور al-fuTuur (*breakfast*.) The more general verb يأكُل ya'kul is used with food items, or in this case, a location phrase.

أحمَد يَتَناوَل الفُطور.	'aHmad yatanaawal al fuTuur.	*Ahmad is eating breakfast.*
مُنى تَشرَب الشاي.	munaa tashrab ash-shaay.	*Mona is drinking tea.*
مُصْطفى يأكُل في المَطْعَم.	muSTafaa ya'kul fi l-maTxam.	*Mustafa is eating at the restaurant.*

Take It Further: Arabic Script

Turn to your script guide to cover yet another group of Arabic letters. This time you'll take a look at two groups, so go to Part 1: Reading Arabic, and read:

- Group 8: ع x and غ gh
- Group 9: ف f and ق q

Vocabulary Builder 2

Track: Lesson 7 Vocabulary Builder 2 (Track 18) CD: 2

May I have ...?	مُمْكِن	mumkin ...?
I will have ...	سأتَناوَل	sa-'atanaawal ...
I would like ...	أُريد	'uriid ...
delicious	شَهيّ	shahiyy
meat	لَحْم	laHm
chicken	دَجاج	dajaaj
rice	أَرُزّ	'aruzz
vegetables	خُضْروات	khuDrawaat
soup	شوربة	shuurba
bread	خُبْز	khubz
salad	سَلَطة	salaTa
dessert	حَلوى	Halwaa
glass	كوب	kuub
cup	فِنجان	finjaan
plate	طَبَق	Tabaq
spoon	مِلْعَقة	milxaqa
fork	شَوكة	shawka
knife	سِكّين	sikkiin

Vocabulary Practice 2

Translate the following into English.

1. سَلَطة salaTa ______
2. خُبْز khubz ______
3. حَلوى Halwaa ______
4. خُضْرَوات khuDrawaat ______
5. أَرُزّ 'aruzz ______
6. شوربة shuurba ______
7. شَوكة shawka ______
8. طَبَق Tabaq ______

ANSWER KEY

1. *salad*; 2. *bread*; 3. *dessert*; 4. *vegetables*; 5. *rice*; 6. *soup*; 7. *fork*; 8. *plate*

Grammar Builder 2

Track: Lesson 7 Grammar Builder 2 (Track 19) CD: 2

POLITE REQUESTS

You've just learned some important expressions you can use as polite requests in eating situations and here they are again:

مُمكِن	mumkin ...?	*May I have ... ?*
سأتَناوَل	sa-'atanaawal ...	*I will have ...*
أُريد	'uriid ...	*I would like ...*

Let's see some examples.

مُمكِن قائمة الطَعام مِن فَضْلَك؟	mumkin qaa'imat aT-Taxaam min faDlak?	*May I have the menu, please?*
سَأتَناوَل شورْبة الخُضْرَوات.	sa-'atanaawal shuurbat al-khuDrawaat.	*I will have the vegetable soup.*
وَأُريدُ أَيْضاً أَن أَطْلُبَ الدجاج المَشويّ.	wa 'uriidu 'ayDan 'an 'aTluba ad-dajaaj al-mashwiyy.	*I would also like to order the grilled chicken.*
هَل تُريدين أَرُزّ أو سَلَطة مَعَ الدَجاج؟	hal turiidiin 'aruzz 'aw salaTa maxa d-dajaaj?	*Would you (f.) like rice or salad with the chicken?*

Did you notice the particle أَن 'an in the third example above? Remember that Arabic doesn't have *to*-infinitives, so to express something like *I would like to order* ..., use the formula (from right to left of course!):

أَطْلُبَ	أَن	أُرِيدُ
'aTluba	'an	'uriidu
I order	*that*	*I would like*

Notice the -a ending on أَطْلُبَ 'aTluba. You know that -u is sometimes used with the regular present tense, unless it's dropped. The -a ending is the ending for a special form of the present called the subjunctive, which is used after the particle أَن 'an. Again, don't worry too much about the subjunctive at this point in your Arabic studies, but learn to recognize it when you see it.

Do you remember the preposition في fi (*in*) from previous lessons? You can use it here to say things like:

الماء في الكوب.	al-maa' fi-l kuub	*The water is in the glass.*

And you already know that prepositions sometimes blend into the definite article ال al as in:

في الفنجان	fi l-finjaan	*in the cup*
في المَطعَم	fi l-maTxam	*at the restaurant*

And just to refresh your memory about gender agreement, the feminine form of the adjective شَهيّ shahiyy (*delicious*) is شَهيّة shahiyya. So, for example, we would say:

لَحْم شَهيّ	laHm shahiyy	*delicious meat*
شوربة شَهيّة	shuurba shahiyya	*delicious soup*

Work Out 1

Track: Lesson 7 Work Out 1 (Track 20) CD: 2

Listen to your audio and fill in the missing words in the following sentences.

1. *This is a good restaurant for dinner.*

   هذا ________________ جيِّد للعَشاء.

   haadhaa ________________ jayyid li l-xashaa'.

2. *I will have the coffee at the café.*

   سَأتَناوَل ________________ في المَقهى.

   sa-'atanaawal ________________ fi l-maqhaa.

3. *I would like tea with milk.*

   أُريدُ شاي ________________.

   'uriidu shaay ________________.

4. *The water is in the glass.*

   ________________ في الكوب.

   ________________ fi l-kuub.

5. *The coffee is in the cup.*

   القَهوة ________________ الفِنجان.

   al-qahwa ________________ l-finjaan.

6. *The sugar is in the coffee.*

السُكَّر ________________.

as-sukkar ________________.

7. *The chicken is delicious.*

________________ شَهيّ.

________________ shahiyy.

This dessert is for dinner.

هذهِ الحلوى ________________.

haadhihi l-Halwaa ________________.

ANSWER KEY

1. مَطْعَم maTxam; 2. القهوة al-qahwa; 3. بالحَليب bi l-Haliib; 4. الماء al-maa'; 5. في fi; 6. في القهوة fi l-qahwa; 7. الدَجاج ad-dajaaj; 8. لِلعَشاء li l-xashaa'

Bring It All Together

Track: Lesson 7 Bring It All Together (Track 21) CD: 2

Now let's bring it all together in a dialogue and add a little bit more vocabulary and structure.

مُمكِن قائمة الطَعام مِن فَضْلَك؟	mumkin qaa'imat aT-Taxaam min faDlak?	*May I have the menu, please?*
طَبْعاً. هذهِ قائِمة طَعام العَشاء.	Tabxan. haadhihi qaa'imat Taxaam al-xashaa'.	*Of course. Here's the dinner menu.*

شُكْراً. سَأتَناوَل شورْبة الخُضْرَوات.	shukran. sa-'atanaawal shuurbat al-khuDrawaat.	*Thank you. I'll have the vegetable soup.*
أَنْصَحُكِ بِشوربة العَدْس. إنّها أفْضَل في الشِتاء.	'anSaHuki bi shuurbat al-xads. 'innahaa 'afDal fi sh-shitaa'.	*I suggest the lentil soup. It's better in the winter.*
حَسَناً. وَأُريدُ أَيْضاً أَن أَطْلُبَ الدجاج المَشويّ.	Hasanan. wa 'uriidu 'ayDan 'an 'aTluba ad-dajaaj al-mashwiyy.	*All right. I would also like to order the grilled chicken.*
إختيار جَيِّد جِداً! الدَجاج المَشوي شَهيّ. هَل تُريدين أَرُزّ أو سَلَطة مَعَ الدَجاج؟	'ikhtiyaar jayyid jiddan! ad-dajaaj al-mashwiyy shahiyy. hal turiidiin 'aruzz 'aw salaTa maxa d-dajaaj?	*A very good choice! The grilled chicken is delicious. Would you like rice or salad with the chicken?*
سَلَطة مِن فَضْلَك. وَإذا سَمَحت ، كوب ماء وَبَعض الخُبْز.	salaTa min faDlak. wa 'idhaa samaHt, kuub maa' wa baxD al-khubz.	*A salad, please. And if possible, a glass of water and some bread.*
بالتأكيد. هَل تُريدين أَنْ تَطلُبي الحَلوى الآن؟	bi t-ta'akiid. hal turiidiin 'an taTlubii l-Halwaa l'aan?	*Certainly. Would you like to order dessert now?*
كَلا. سأتَناوَل فِنجان قَهوة بالحَليب فَقَط بَعْد العَشاء.	kallaa. sa-'atanaawal finjaan qahwa bi l-haliib faqaT baxd al-xashaa'.	*No. I will only have a cup of coffee with milk after dinner.*

Take It Further

Track: Lesson 7 Take It Further (Track 22) CD: 2

Okay, you already have enough knowledge of Arabic that you could probably figure out the meanings of all the new words you just heard, but let's go over them just in case:

أَنْصَحُكِ	'anSaHuki	*I recommend (to you (f.))*
أَفْضَل	'afDal	*better*
في الشِتاء	fi sh-shitaa'	*in the winter*
حَسَناً	Hasanan	*all right*
مَشويّ	mashwiyy	*grilled*
إختيار	'ikhtiyaar	*choice*
إذا سَمَحْت	'idhaa samaHt	*if possible*
بالتأكيد	bi t-ta'kiid	*of course, certainly*
فَقَط	faqaT	*only*
مَعَ	maxa	*with*
مَعَ الدجاج	maxa d-dajaaj	*with the chicken.*

Work Out 2

First, connect the English words or phrases with their Arabic equivalents.

1. *only* — a. بالتأكيد bi t-ta'kiid
2. *please* — b. إخْتيار 'ikhtiyaar
3. *choice* — c. في الشِتاء fi sh-shitaa'
4. *better* — d. مِن فَضْلَك min faDlak
5. *in the winter* — e. فَقَط faqaT
6. *of course* — f. أَفْضَل 'afDal

ANSWERS KEY

1. e; 2. d; 3. b; 4. f; 5. c; 6. a

Now let's practice some of the verbs you've already seen. Study these sentences:

أحمَد يَتَناوَل الفُطور.	'aHmad yatanaawal al-fuTuur.	*Ahmad is eating breakfast.*
مُنى تَشرَب الشاي.	munaa tashrab ash-shaay.	*Mona is drinking tea.*
مُصْطفى يأكُل في المَطْعَم.	muSTafaa ya'kul fi l-maTxam.	*Mustafa is eating at the restaurant.*

And now translate the following:

1. *Ahmad is drinking tea.*

2. *Mustafa is eating breakfast.*

3. *Mona is eating at the restaurant.*

4. *Mustafa is drinking tea at the café.*

5. *Ahmed is eating the chicken.*

ANSWER KEY

1. أحْمد يَشْرَب الشاي. 'aHmad yashrab ash-shaay. 2. مُصطفى يَتَناوَل الفُطور. muSTafaa yatanaawal al-fuTuur. 3. مُنى تأكُل في المَطْعَم. munaa ta'kul fi l-maTxam. 4. مُصْطفى يَشْرَبُ الشاي في المَقهى. muSTafaa yashrabu sh-shaay fi l-maqhaa. 5. أحمَد يأكُلُ الدجاج. 'aHmad ya'kulu d-dajaaj.

Drive It Home

Let's practice those verbs. Change each of the following sentences by substituting the underlined food item with each of the ones in parentheses. Say each new sentence aloud, and write it out as well. The first sentence means: *I'm eating the meat (the chicken, the rice, the bread)*. Then, in the next sentences, you have the pronouns and verb forms for *you* (m.), *you* (f.), *he, she, we, you* (pl. m.), *you* (pl. f.), *they* (m.) and *they* (f.).

1. أنا آكُلُ اللَحم. (الدَجاج، الأرُزّ، الخُبز)

'anaa 'aakulu al-laHm (ad-dajaaj, al-'aruzz, al-khubz)

2. أنتَ تأكُلُ اللَحم. (الدَجاج، الأرُزّ، الخُبْز)

'anta ta'kulu al-laHm (ad-dajaaj, al-'aruzz, al-khubz)

3. أنتِ تأكُلين اللَحم. (الدَجاج، الأرُزّ، الخُبْز)

'anti ta'kuliina al-laHm (ad-dajaaj, al-'aruzz, al-khubz)

4. هوَ يأكُلُ اللَحم. (الدَجاج، الأرُزّ، الخُبْز)

huwa ya'kulu al-laHm (ad-dajaaj, al-'aruzz, al-khubz)

5. هيَ تأكُلُ اللَحم. (الدَجاج، الأرُزّ، الخُبز)

hiya ta'kulu al-laHm (ad-dajaaj, al-'aruzz, al-khubz)

6. نَحْنُ نأْكُلُ اللَحم. (الدَجاج، الأرُزّ، الخُبز)

naHnu na'kulu al-laHm (ad-dajaaj, al-'aruzz, al-khubz)

7. أنتُم تأكُلون اللَحم. (الدَجاج، الأرُزّ، الخُبْز)

'antum ta'kuluuna al-laHm (ad-dajaaj, al-'aruzz, al-khubz)

8. أَنْتُنَّ تَأْكُلْنَ اللَحم. (الدَجاج، الأَرُزّ، الخُبْز)

'antunna ta'kulna al-laHm (ad-dajaaj, al-'aruzz, al-khubz)

9. هُم يأكُلُونَ اللَحم. (الدَجاج، الأَرُزّ، الخُبْز)

hum ya'kuluuna al-laHm (ad-dajaaj, al-'aruzz, al-khubz)

10. هُنَّ يَكُلْنَ اللَحم. (الدَجاج، الأَرُزّ، الخُبْز)

hunna ya'kulna al-laHm (ad-dajaaj, al-'aruzz, al-khubz)

Now, let's try the same thing with *I drink the coffee (the tea, the milk, the water)*.

1. أنا أَشْرَبُ القَهوة. (الشاي، الحَليب، الماء)

'anaa 'ashrabu l-qahwa (ash-shaay, al-Haliib, al-maa')

2. أنتَ تَشْرَبُ القَهوة. (الشاي، الحَليب، الماء)

'anta tashrabu l-qahwa (ash-shaay, al-Haliib, al-maa')

3. أنتِ تَشْرَبينَ القَهوة. (الشاي، الحَليب، الماء)

'anti tashrabiina l-qahwa (ash-shaay, al-Haliib, al-maa')

4. هوَ يَشْرَبُ القَهوة. (الشاي، الحَليب، الماء)

huwa yashrabu l-qahwa (ash-shaay, al-Haliib, al-maa')

5. هيَ تَشْرَبُ القَهوة. (الشاي، الحَليب، الماء)

hiya tashrabu l-qahwa (ash-shaay, al-Haliib, al-maa')

6. نَحْنُ نَشْرَبُ القَهوة. (الشاي، الحَليب، الماء)

naHnu nashrabu l-qahwa (ash-shaay, al-Haliib, al-maa')

7. أنتُم تَشْرَبُون القَهوة. (الشاي، الحَليب، الماء)

'antum tashrabuuna l-qahwa (ash-shaay, al-Haliib, al-maa')

8. أنتُنَّ تَشْرَبْنَ القَهوة. (الشاي، الحَليب، الماء)

'antunna tashrabna l-qahwa (ash-shaay, al-Haliib, al-maa')

9. هُم يَشْرَبون القَهوة. (الشاي، الحَليب، الماء)

hum yashrabuuna l-qahwa (ash-shaay, al-Haliib, al-maa')

10. هُنَّ يَشْرَبنَ القَهوة. (الشاي، الحَليب، الماء)

hunna yashrabna l-qahwa (sh-shaay, a-Haliib, al-maa')

Take It Further: Arabic Script

Turn back to your script guide to practice writing the letters you learned earlier in the lesson. Go to Part 2: Writing Arabic, and complete:

- Group 8: ع and غ
- Group 9: ف and ق

Parting Words

عَظيم! xaDHiim! *Great!* You've finished another lesson. In this lesson, you learned a lot of essential vocabulary related to one of the great joys of traveling and experiencing a new culture—eating! By now, you should know:

- ☐ Basic vocabulary for meals. (Still unsure? Go back to 144.)
- ☐ How to say the names of common food and drink items. (Still unsure? Go back to 146.)
- ☐ Important vocabulary for use in a restaurant. (Still unsure? Go back to 148.)
- ☐ Key phrases for ordering food. (Still unsure? Go back to 149.)
- ☐ How to put it all together in a dialogue about ordering a meal. (Still unsure? Go back to 153.)

Don't forget to practice and reinforce what you've learned by visiting **www.livinglanguage.com/languagelab** for flashcards, games, and quizzes.

Culture Note

Did you know that during the Muslim holy month of Ramadan, many Muslims observe a complete fast and do not eat or drink anything from sunrise to sunset? Also during Ramadan, you will hear that dinner – العَشاء al-xashaa' – is referred to as breakfast – الإفْطار al-'ifTaar – because it's the first meal of the day after the fast is broken at sunset. The month of Ramadan is followed by a holiday called عيد الفِطْر xiid al-fiTr, a three day celebration during which it is customary to visit your friends and relatives and enjoy many big meals together. وَجْبة هَنيَّة wajba haniyya! *Have a nice meal!*

Word Recall

Choose an adjective that can be used to describe the noun in each question, then translate into English. Not all choices given are adjectives:-

1. غُرفة نَوم ghurfat nawm
   a. واسِع waasix
   b. صَغيرة Saghiira
   c. بَعيد baxiid
2. شارِع shaarix
   a. واسِع waasix
   b. مَكْتَب البَريد maktab al-bariid
   c. سَيّارة أُجرة sayyarat 'ujra
3. حديقة Hadiiqa
   a. جميلة jamiila
   b. أَحْمَر 'aHmar
   c. غُرْفَة طَعام ghurfat Taxaam
4. نِساء nisaa'
   a. مَدْرَسة madrasa
   b. طَويلات Tawiilaat
   c. زَرْقاء zarqaa'
5. عُنوان xunwaan
   a. سَوْداء sawdaa'
   b. قَريب qariib
   c. واسِعة waasixa
6. طِفلة Tifla
   a. بَعيدة مِن baxiida min
   b. يأكُلون ya'kuluun
   c. جَميلة jamiila
7. مُدَرِّس mudarris
   a. عُنوان xunwaan
   b. يَسْكُن yaskun
   c. سَعيد saxiid

8. دَجاج **dajaaj**

a. شَهيّ **shahiyy**

b. واسِع **waasix**

c. طِوال **Tiwaal**

9. إختيار **'ikhtiyaar**

a. فُنْدُق **funduq**

b. جَيِّد **jayyid**

c. زَرقاء **zarqaa'**

10. الجامِعة **al-jaamixa**

a. سُعَداء **suxadaa'**

b. جَميل **jamiil**

c. القَريبة **al-qariiba**

ANSWER KEY

1. b (*a small bedroom*); 2. a (*a wide street*); 3. a (*a beautiful garden*); 4. b (*tall women*); 5. b (*a nearby/close address*); 6. c (*a beautiful child*); 7. c (*a happy teacher*); 8. a (*delicious chicken*); 9. b (*a good choice*); 10.c (*the nearby/close university*)

Lesson 8: Everyday life

الدَرس الثامِن: الحياة اليَومية

ad-dars ath-thaamin: al-Hayaa l-yawmiyya

أهلاً وَسَهلاً ahlan wa sahlan! *Welcome!* In this lesson, you'll learn more vocabulary and structures that will help you communicate with others about everyday life. You'll learn:

- ☐ the seasons of the year
- ☐ how to give commands
- ☐ vocabulary for talking about the weather
- ☐ how to form negative sentences
- ☐ how to put it all together in a short conversation about planning around the weather

As always, we'll start with some new vocabulary. هيّا نبدأ hayya nabdaa' *Let's begin!*

Vocabulary Builder 1

Track: Lesson 8 Vocabulary Builder 1 (Track 23) CD: 2

today	اليَوم	al-yawm
week	أُسْبوع	'usbuux

month	شَهْر	shahr
summer	الصَيْف	aS-Sayf
spring	الرَبيع	ar-rabiix
fall	الخَريف	al-khariif
winter	الشِتاء	ash-shitaa'
weather	جَوّ	jaww
always	دائماً	daa'iman
sometimes	أحياناً	aHyaanan
at all	على الإطْلاق	xala-l 'iTlaaq
newspaper	جَريدة	jariida
news	أَخبار	'akhbaar
according to	حَسَب	Hasab
museum	مَتْحَف	matHaf
theater	مَسْرَح	masraH
great idea	فِكرة هائِلة	fikra haa'ila

Vocabulary Practice 1

Match the English word with its Arabic equivalent:

1. *summer* — a. شَهر shahr
2. *fall* — b. مَتْحَف matHaf

3. *newspaper* c. الصيْف aS-Sayf

4. *month* d. أُسبوع 'usbuux

5. *week* e. الخَريف al-khariif

6. *museum* f. جَريدة jariida

ANSWER KEY

1. c; 2. e; 3. f; 4. a; 5. d; 6. b

Now let's practice reading some Arabic script. Can you pronounce and translate these words?

1. دائماً ______________

2. أحياناً ______________

3. فِكرة هائِلة ______________

4. الشِتاء ______________

5. جَوّ ______________

ANSWER KEY

1. daa'iman (*always*); 2. 'aHyaanan (*sometimes*); 3. fikra haa'ila (*great idea*); 4. ash-shitaa' (*winter*); 5. jaww (*weather*)

Grammar Builder 1

Track: Lesson 8 Grammar Builder 1 (Track 24) CD: 2

INTRODUCTION TO COMMANDS

Now let's talk a bit about the imperative forms of Arabic verbs used to give commands and make requests. Imperatives are formed by adding a vowel to the beginning of the verbs, in place of the prefixes that you already know. There are three forms of the imperative:

FORM	USE
masculine	*when addressing a man*
feminine	*when addressing a woman*
plural	*when addressing more than one person*

In addition to the vowel at the beginning, the feminine form also takes the ending ي -ii and the plural form takes the ending وا -uu. (Note that ا is silent.) Let's take the verb يَذْهَب yadhhab (*go*), as an example.

إذْهَب	'idhhab	*Go. (masculine singular)*
إذْهَبي	'idhhabii	*Go. (feminine singular)*
إذْهَبوا	'idhabuu	*Go. (plural)*

Take It Further: Arabic Script

Turn to your script guide to cover yet another group of Arabic letters. This time you'll take a look at four consonants that you're no doubt familiar with by now. Go to Part 1: Reading Arabic, and read:

- Group 10: ك k, ل l, م m, and ن n

Vocabulary Builder 2

Track: Lesson 8 Vocabulary Builder 2 (Track 25) CD: 2

the weather forecast	النَشرة الجَويّة	an-nashra l-jawiyya
warm	دافِئ	daafi'
hot	حارّ	Haarr
cold	بارِد	baarid
pleasant	لَطيف	laTiif
refreshing	منعش	munxish
sun	شَمْس	shams
moon	قَمَر	qamar
rain	مَطَر	maTar
rainy	مُمطِر	mumTir
wind	رِياح	riyaaH
strong	شَديد	shadiid
mild, moderate	مُعْتَدِل	muxtadil

dry	جاف	jaaff
nature	الطَبيعة	aT-Tabiixa

Vocabulary Practice 2

Let's take this opportunity to practice reading some Arabic script. Translate each of the following into English. You'll see the transcription along with the correct answer:

1. لَطيف ________________
2. جافّ ________________
3. شَمْس ________________
4. دافِئ ________________
5. بارِد ________________
6. حارّ ________________

ANSWER KEY:

1. *pleasant,* laTiif; 2. *dry,* jaaff; 3. *sun,* shams; 4. *warm,* daafi'; 5. *cold,* baarid; 6. *hot,* Haarr

Grammar Builder 2

Track: Lesson 8 Grammar Builder 2 (Track 26) CD: 2

INTRODUCTION TO NEGATIVES

If you want to say that the weather is *not warm*, you use لَيْسَ laysa (*is not*) directly before the adjective. لَيْسَ laysa is the masculine singular form, and لَيْسَت laysat is the feminine singular.

Masculine: ...الجَوّ al-jaww ... (*The weather ...*)

لَيسَ دافِئ.	laysa daafi'.	*is not warm.*
لَيْس حارّ.	laysa Haarr.	*is not hot.*

Feminine: ...المَدينة al-madiina ... (*The city ...*)

لَيْسَت دافِئة.	laysat daafi'a.	*is not warm.*
لَيْسَت حارّة.	laysat Haarra.	*is not hot.*

You already know that the verb *to be* is not expressed in Arabic. But that's actually only the case for the present tense affirmative. *To be* is expressed in the negative, and also in the past and future, but we'll leave that for future lessons. For now, take a look at a few other examples of negative *to be* sentences in the present.

مَكتَبُها لَيسَ بَعيد.	maktabuhaa laysa baxiid.	*Her office is not far.*
الرياح ليست شَديدة.	ar-riyaaH laysat shadiida.	*The wind is not strong.*
البِنْتُ لَيْسَتْ فِي البُسْتَان.	al-bint laysat fi l-bustaan.	*The girl is not in the garden.*

With other verbs, use the particle لا la (*not*) directly before the conjugated form.

لا أذهَبُ.	laa 'adhhabu.	*I do not go.*
لا أتَكَلَّم اللُغة العَرَبية.	laa 'atakallam al-lugha al-xarabiyya.	*I don't speak Arabic.*

Negatives can get a bit tricky in Arabic, with different negative particles and different forms of the verb used depending on tense. But don't worry; you'll get to that eventually. For now, this is a good introduction.

Work Out 1

Track: Lesson 8 Work Out 1 (Track 27) CD: 2

Listen to your audio and fill in the missing words in the following sentences.

1. *Spring is warm.*

________ دافِئ.

________ daafi'.

2. *Summer is hot.*

________ حارّ.

________ Haarr.

3. *Fall is not warm.*

الخَريف ________ دافِئ.

al-khariif ________ daafi'.

4. *Winter is not hot.*

الشِتاء لَيْسَ ________.

ash-shitaa' laysa ________.

5. *The wind is strong.*

________ شَديدة.

________ shadiida.

6. *The weather is pleasant.*

الجَوّ ________.

al-jaww ________.

7. *Today's newspaper*

جَريدة ________

jariidat ________

8. *This is not a theater.*

هَذا لَيْسَ ________________.

haadhaa laysa ________________.

9. *This is a museum.*

هذا ________________.

haadhaa ________________.

ANSWER KEY

1. الرَبيع **ar-rabiix**; 2. الصَيْف **aS-Sayf**; 3. لَيْسَ **laysa**; 4. حارّ **Haarr**; 5. الرِياح **ar-riyaaH**; 6. لَطيف **laTiif**; 7. اليَوم **al-yawm**; 8. مَسْرَح **masraH**; 9. مَتْحَف **matHaf**

Bring It All Together

Track: Lesson 8 Bring It All Together (Track 28) CD: 2

Now let's bring it all together and add a little bit more vocabulary and structure.

أهلا مُنى! الجَوّ لَطيف اليَوم.	**'ahlan munaa! al-jaww laTiif al-yawm.**	*Hello, Mona! The weather is pleasant today.*
نَعَم يا طارِق. إنَّ الشَمْس دافِئة جِدّاً اليَوْم.	**naxam, yaa Taariq, inna sh-shams daafi'a jiddan al-yawm.**	*Yes, Tareq, the sun is very warm today.*
وَالرياح ليست شَديدة.	**wa r-riyaaH laysat shadiida.**	*And the wind is not strong.*
كلاّ إنّها مُنْعِشة!	**kallaa, innahaa munxisha!**	*No, it's refreshing!*

حَسَب النَشرة الجويّة في الجَريدة الجَوّهذا الأُسبوع مُعْتَدِل.	Hasab an-nashra al-jawiyya fi l-jariida, al-jaww haadha l-usbuux muxtadil.	*According to the weather forecast in the newspaper, the weather will be mild this week.*
الربيع في بَيروت دائماً مُعتَدِل.	ar-rabiix fi bayruut daa'iman muxtadil.	*Spring in Beirut is always mild.*
وَلَيْسَ مُمْطِر على الإطْلاق!	wa laysa mumTir xala l-'iTlaaq!	*And not rainy at all!*
لكِن الشِتاء أحياناً مُمْطِر وَبارِد.	laakin ash-shitaa' aHyanan mumTir wa baarid.	*But the winter is sometimes rainy and cold.*
في الشِتاء أُحِبُّ أن أذهَب إلى المَتْحَف أو إلى المَسْرَح.	fi sh-shitaa' 'uHibbu 'an 'adhhab 'ila l-matHaf 'aw 'ila l-masraH.	*In the winter, I like to go to the museum or the theater.*
وَلكن اليَوم هيّا نَسْتَمتِع بالطَبيعة!	wa laakin al-yawm hayyaa nastamtix bi T-Tabiixa!	*But today let's enjoy nature!*
فِكرة هائلة!	fikra haa'ila!	*Great idea!*

Work Out 2

Translate each of the following adjectival sentences, then give the negative forms with لَيْسَ laysa or لَيْسَت laysat.

1. الجَوّ دافِئ. al-jaww daafi'.

2. الصَيْف حارّ. aS-Sayf Haarr.

3. الشِتاء بارِد. ash-shitaa' baarid.

4. الرَبيع لَطيف. ar-rabiix laTiif.

5. الرِياح شَديدة. ar-riyaaH shadiida.

ANSWER KEY

1. *The weather is warm.* (لجَوّ لَيْسَا دافِئ al-jaww lasya daafi') 2. *The summer is hot.* (الصَيْف لَيْسَ حارّ aS-Sayf laysa Haarr) 3. *The winter is cold.* (الشِتاء لَيْسَ بارِد ash-shitaa' laysa baarid) 4. *The spring is pleasant.* (الرَبيع لَيْسَ لَطيف ar-rabiix laysa laTiif) 5. *The wind is strong.* (الرِياح لَيْسَت شَديدة ar-riyaaH laysat shadiida)

Now let's practice negating sentences with verbs. Give the present negative with laa لا and then translate each answer.

1. أذهب إلى المَتْحَف. 'adhhab 'ilaa l-matHaf.

2. أذهب إلى المَسْرَح. 'adhhab 'ilaa l-masraH.

3. أذهب إلى المَطْعَم. 'adhhab 'ilaa l-maTxam.

4. أذهب إلى المقهى. 'adhhab 'ilaa l-maqhaa.

ANSWER KEY

1. .لا أذهب إلى المَتْحَف laa 'adhhab 'ilaa l-matHaf. *(I am not going to the museum.)* 2. .لا أذهب إلى المَسْرَح laa 'adhhab 'ilaa l-masraH. *(I am not going to the theater.)* 3. .لا أذهب إلى المَطْعَم laa 'adhhab 'ilaa l-maTxam. *(I am not going to the restaurant.)* 4. .لا أذهب إلى المقهى laa 'adhhab 'ilaa l-maqhaa. *(I am not going to the café.)*

Drive It Home

Let's get in some more practice with verbs, including negatives. Just as you did in Lesson 7, rewrite each sentence by replacing the underlined phrase with each of the new phrases in parentheses. The first sentence means *I'm going to the restaurant. (to the café, to the theater, to the museum)*. The following sentences use the other personal pronouns you've learned.

1. أنا أذْهَب إلى المَطْعَم. (إلى المَقهى، إلى المَسْرَح، إلى المَتْحَف)

'anaa 'adhhabu 'ila l-maTxam. ('ila l-maqhaa, 'ila l-masraH, 'ila l-matHaf.)

---

2. أنتَ تَذْهَب إلى المَطْعَم. (إلى المَقهى، إلى المَسْرَح، إلى المَتْحَف)

'anta tadhhabu 'ila l-maTxam. ('ila l-maqhaa, 'ila l-masraH, 'ila l-matHaf.)

---

3. أَنْتِ تَذْهبينَ إلى المَطْعَم. (إلى المَقهى، إلى المَسْرَح، إلى المَتْحَف)

'anti tadhhabiina 'ila l-maTxam. ('ila l-maqhaa, 'ila l-masraH, 'ila l-matHaf.)

---

4. هوَ يَذْهَبُ إلى المَطْعَم. (إلى المَقهى، إلى المَسْرَح، إلى المَتْحَف)

huwa yadhhabu 'ila l-maTxam. ('ila l-maqhaa, 'ila l-masraH, 'ila l-matHaf.)

---

5. هيَ تَذهَبُ إلى المَطْعَم. (إلى المَقهى، إلى المَسْرَح، إلى المَتْحَف)

hiya tadhhabu 'ila l-maTxam. ('ila l-maqhaa, 'ila l-masraH, 'ila l-matHaf.)

6. نَحْنُ نَذْهَبُ إلى المَطْعَم. (إلى المَقهى، إلى المَسْرَح، إلى المَتْحَف)

naHnu nadhhabu 'ila l-maTxam. ('ila l-maqhaa, 'ila l-masraH, 'ila l-matHaf.)

أَنْتُم تَذهَبونَ إلى المَطْعَم. (إلى المَقهى، إلى المَسْرَح، إلى المَتْحَف)

'antum tadhhabuuna 'ila l-maTxam. ('ila l-maqhaa, 'ila l-masraH, 'ila l-matHaf.)

7. أَنْتُنَّ تَذْهَبْنَ إلى المَطْعَم. (إلى المَقهى، إلى المَسْرَح، إلى المَتْحَف)

'antunna tadhhabna 'ila l-maTxam. ('ila l-maqha, 'ila l-masraH, 'ila l-matHaf.)

8. هُم يَذْهَبون إلى المَطْعَم. (إلى المَقهى، إلى المَسْرَح، إلى المَتْحَف)

hum yadhhabuuna 'ila l-maTxam. ('ila l-maqhaa, 'ila l-masraH, 'ila l-matHaf.)

9. هُنَّ يَذهَبنَ إلى المَطْعَم. (إلى المَقهى، إلى المَسْرَح، إلى المَتْحَف)

hunna yadhhabna 'ila l-maTxam. ('ila l-maqhaa, 'ila l-masraH, 'ila l-matHaf.)

Now, practice the negative by re-stating each sentence with إلى المَطْعَم 'ilaa l-maTxam, including لا laa before the verb.

Take It Further: Arabic Script

Turn back to your script guide to practice writing the letters you learned earlier in this lesson. Go to Part 2: Writing Arabic, and complete:

- Group 10: ك, ل, م, and ن

Parting Words

رائع raa'ix! *Wonderful!* You've completed one more lesson, and by now you should know:

- ☐ the seasons of the year. (Still unsure? Go back to 165.)
- ☐ how to give commands. (Still unsure? Go back to 168.)
- ☐ vocabulary for talking about the weather. (Still unsure? Go back to 169.)
- ☐ how to form negative sentences. (Still unsure? Go back to 171.)
- ☐ how to put it all together in a short conversation about planning around the weather. (Still unsure? Go back to 174.)

Don't forget to practice and reinforce what you've learned by visiting **www.livinglanguage.com/languagelab** for flashcards, games, and quizzes.

Take It Further

Track: Lesson 8 Take It Further (Track 29) CD: 2

Did you know that a number of Arab countries, for religious and sometimes also civil purposes, follow a calendar that is different from the Gregorian calendar used in the United States? The Islamic Hijri calendar, or التقويم الهِجريّ at-taqwiim al-hijriyy, is calculated from the year AD 622, when the prophet Mohammed emigrated to Mecca. And while the names of the Gregorian calendar months in Arabic are very similar to their European counterparts—for example, ينايِر yanaayir for *January,* فِبراير fibraayir for *February,* and مارِس maaris for *March*—the months of the Islamic calendar have very different names, like مُحَرَّم muHarram for the first month of the year, صَفَر Safar for the second month, and رَبيع الأوَّل rabiix al-'awwal for the third month.

إلى اللِقاء 'ilaa l-liqaa'! *Till next time!*

Word Recall

Choose a, b, or c to make a logical phrase or sentence, then translate your answers.

1. مَطار maTaar
   a. واسِعة waasixa
   b. صَغير Saghiir
   c. شَهر shahr
2. الفُندُق al-funduq
   a. لَطيف laTiif
   b. مَكْتَب البَريد maktab al-bariid
   c. سَيّارة أُجرة sayyarat 'ujra
3. صَيدَليّة Saydaliyya
   a. قَريبة qariiba
   b. أَحْمَر 'aHmar
   c. غُرْفَة طَعام ghurfat Taxaam
4. أَبْحَثُ عَن 'abHathu xan
   a. شارِع shaarix
   b. طَويلات Tawiilaat
   c. زَرْقاء zarqaa'
5. نَتَناوَلُ natanaawalu
   a. الفُطور al-fuTuur
   b. قَريب qariib
   c. واسِعة waasixa
6. الصَيف aS-Sayf
   a. سُكَّر sukkar
   b. يأكُلون ya'kuluun
   c. دافِئ daafi'
7. يأكُلُ ya'kulu
   a. عُنوان xunwaan
   b. دجاج dajaaj
   c. سَعيد saxiid

8. الجَوّ al-jaww

a. شَهيّ shahiyy
b. مُعتَدِل muxtadil
c. طِوال Tiwaal

9. أَذهَبُ إلى 'adhhabu 'ilaa

a. الفُنْدُق al-funduq
b. جَيِّد jayyid
c. زَرقاء zarqaa'

10. الأخبار al-'akhbaar

a. قَمَر qamar
b. جَميل jamiil
c. في الجَريدة fi l-jariida

ANSWER KEY

1. b (*a small airport*); 2. a (*The hotel is pleasant.*) 3. a (*a nearby pharmacy*); 4. a (*I'm searching for a street.*) 5. a (*We are having breakfast.*) 6. a (*Summer is warm.*) 7. b (*He eats chicken.*) 8. b (*The weather is mild.*) 9. a (*I am going to the hotel.*) 10. c (*The news is in the newspaper.*)

Lesson 9: At Work

ألدَرس ألتاسِع : في العَمل

ad-dars at-taasix: fi l-xamal

كَيْف الحال؟ kayf al-Haal? *How are you?* In this lesson, you'll learn:

- □ the names of the days of the week
- □ how to use them along with other time expressions
- □ how to ask what time it is
- □ important vocabulary related to time and routines
- □ how to use it all in a conversation related to the workplace

Are you ready to begin your second-to-last lesson?

Vocabulary Builder 1

Track: Lesson 9 Vocabulary Builder 1 (Track 30) CD: 2

Monday	الإثنين	al-'ithnayn
Tuesday	الثلاثاء	ath-thulaathaa'
Wednesday	الأربعاء	al-'arbaxaa'
Thursday	الخَميس	al-khamiis
Friday	الجُمعة	al-jumxa

Saturday	السَبْت	as-sabt
Sunday	الأحَد	al-'aHad
tomorrow	غداً	ghadan
yesterday	البارِحة - بِالأمس	al-baariHa, bi l-'ams
noon	الظُهر	aDH-DHuhr
afternoon	بَعد الظُهر	baxd aDH-DHuhr
night	الليل	al-layl

Vocabulary Practice 1

Match the following English words with their Arabic translations.

1. *Friday* — a. الليل al-layl
2. *yesterday* — b. الخميس al-khamiis
3. *noon* — c. البارِحة al-baariHa
4. *tomorrow* — d. غَداً ghadan
5. *Thursday* — e. الظُهر aDH-DHuhr
6. *night* — f. الجُمعة al-jumxa

ANSWER KEY

1. f; 2. c; 3. e; 4. d; 5. b; 6. a

Grammar Builder 1

Track: Lesson 9 Grammar Builder 1 (Track 31) CD: 2

DAYS AND TIME EXPRESSIONS

Let's review the days of the week in Arabic. Notice that *Sunday* through *Thursday* are based on the numbers one through five.

الأحَد	al-'aHad	*Sunday*
الإثنين	al-'ithnayn	*Monday*
الثُلاثاء	ath-thulaathaa'	*Tuesday*
الأربعاء	al-'arbaxaa'	*Wednesday*
الخَميس	al-khamiis	*Thursday*
الجُمعة	al-jumxa	*Friday*
السَبْت	as-sabt	*Saturday*

To say that you do something on a particular day of the week, you can use the name of the day, preceded by the word يَوم yawm (*day*). For example, *Monday* or *on Monday* is يَوم الإثنين yawm al-'ithnayn.

أعْمَل يَوم الإثنين.	'axmal yawm al-'ithnayn.	*I work on Monday.*
لا أعْمَل يَوم السَبْت.	laa 'axmal yawm as-sabt.	*I don't work on Saturday.*

Other useful terms related to days are:

غداً	ghadan	*tomorrow*
البارِحة	al-baariHa	*yesterday*
الظُهْر	aDH-DHuhr	*noon*
بَعْد الظُهر	baxd aDH-DHuhr	*afternoon*
الليل	al-layl	*night*

Don't forget the words صَباح SabaaH (*morning*) and مَساء masaa' (*evening*) from Lesson 1, and the word أُسبوع 'usbuux (*week*) from Lesson 8.

Now, let's add a couple more useful words. ماضي maaDi means *last* or *in the past*, and قادِم qaadim means *next*, or *in the future*.

الإثنين الماضي	al-'ithnayn al-maaDi	*last Monday*
الإثنَين القادِم	al-'ithnayn al-qaadim	*next Monday*

Take It Further: Arabic Script

Turn to your script guide to cover yet another group of Arabic letters. Go to *Part 1: Reading Arabic*, and read:

- Group 11: ه h and ة taa' marbuuTa

Vocabulary Builder 2

Track: Lesson 9 Vocabulary Builder 2 (Track 32) CD: 2

What time is it?	كَم الساعة؟	kam as-saaxa?
It's ... o'clock.	الساعة	as-saaxa ...
when	مَتى	mataa
hour, clock, watch	ساعة	saaxa
minute	دقيقة	daqiiqa
year	سنة	sana
half	نِصف	niSf
quarter	رُبْع	rubx
soon	قَريباً	qariiban
never	أَبَداً	'abadan
every day	كُلَّ يوم	kulla yawm

Vocabulary Practice 2

Can you recall what the following Arabic words/phrases mean in English?

1. أَبَداً 'abadan ________________
2. نِصف niSf ________________
3. كَم الساعة؟ kam as-saaxa? ________________
4. دقيقة daqiiqa ________________

5. كُلَّ يَوم kulla yawm ______________

6. قَريباً qariiban ______________

ANSWER KEY

1. *never;* 2. *half;* 3. *What time is it?* 4. *minute;* 5. *every day;* 6. *soon*

Grammar Builder 2

Track: Lesson 9 Grammar Builder 2 (Track 1) CD: 3

TELLING TIME

When giving the time in Arabic, you use ordinal numbers like *first, second, third,* and so on. So, *two o'clock* is literally *the second hour*. Let's look at the ordinals from *first* through *twelfth* now. Keep in mind that you'll use the feminine forms with الساعة as-saaxa (*the hour*), which is of course a feminine noun ending in ة -a.

أوَّل ، أولى	'awwal, 'uulaa	*first (m., f.)*
ثاني ، ثانية	thaanii, thaaniya	*second (m., f.)*
ثالِث ، ثالِثة	thaalith, thaalitha	*third (m., f.)*
رابِع ، رابِعة	raabix, raabixa	*fourth (m., f.)*
خامِس ، خامِسة	khaamis, khaamisa	*fifth (m., f.)*
سادِس ، سادِسة	saadis, saadisa	*sixth (m., f.)*
سابِع ، سابِعة	saabix, saabixa	*seventh (m., f.)*
ثامِن ، ثامِنة	thaamin, thaamina	*eighth (m., f.)*
تاسِع ، تاسِعة	taasix, taasixa	*ninth (m., f.)*

عاشِر، عاشِرة	xaashir, xaashira	*tenth (m., f.)*
حادي عَشَر، حادية عشرة	Haadii xaashar, Haadiyata xashra	*eleventh (m., f.)*
ثاني عَشَر، ثانية عَشْرة	thaanii xaashar, thaaniyata xashra	*twelfth (m., f.)*

Now that you know ordinal numbers, we can take a look at how to tell time. One point to keep in mind is that you'll use واحِدة waaHida instead of أولى 'uulaa (*first*) when saying one o'clock. To give the time, start with الساعة ... as-saaxa ... (*It's ... o'clock*, literally, *The time is ...*).

الساعة الواحِدة.	as-saaxa l-waaHida.	*It's one o'clock.*
الساعة الثانية.	as-saaxa th-thaaniya.	*It's two o'clock.*
الساعة السابِعة.	as-saaxa s-saabixa.	*It's seven o'clock.*

To say it's half past an hour, use وَالنِصف wa n-niSf (*and the half.*) To say it's a quarter past an hour, use وَالرُبع wa r-rubx (*and the quarter*).

الساعة العاشِرة وَالنِصف.	as-saaxa l-xaashira wa n-niSf.	*It's 10:30.*
الساعة الخامِسة وَالرُبع.	as-saaxa l-khaamisa wa r-rubux.	*It's 5:15.*

To say that it's a certain number of minutes after the hour, use و wa (*and*), plus the number, followed by دقائق daqaa'iq (*minutes*). To say that it's a certain number of minutes before the hour, use إلاّ 'illaa (*to, until*).

الساعة الثانية وَعَشر دقائق.	as- saaxa ath-thaaniya wa xashar daqaa'iq.	*It's 2:10.*
الساعة الثانية إلاّ عَشَر دقائق.	as- saaxa ath-thaaniya 'illaa xashar daqaa'iq	*It's 1:50.*

By now you know how to form questions using مَتى mataa (*when*), so let's review some common, useful time expressions you can use in answering questions with مَتى mataa (*when*).

ساعة	saaxa	*hour*
دقيقة	daqiiqa	*minute*
دقائق	daqaa'iq	*minutes*
سنة	sana	*year*
نِصف	niSf	*half*
رُبع	rubx	*quarter*
تماماً	tamaaman	*exactly*
حَوالي	Hawaalii	*approximately*
قَريباً	qariiban	*soon*
أبَداً	'abadan	*never*

كُلَّ يَوم	kulla yawm	*every day, daily*
أحياناً	'aHyaanan	*sometimes*
مُنتَصَف اللَيْل	muntaSaf al-layl	*midnight*
بَيْن	bayna	*between*
صَباحاً	SabaaHan	*in the morning*
مساءً	masaa'an	*in the evening*

Work Out 1

Listen to your audio, and fill in the missing words in the sentences below. Notice that expressions such as *at noon*, *in the morning*, and *in the evening* add -(a)n to the nouns: صَباح SabaaH means *morning*, and صَباحاً SabaaHan means *in the morning*.

Track: Lesson 9 Work Out 1 (Track 2) CD: 3

1. *What time is it?*

   كَم ______؟

   kam ______?

2. *It's exactly ten o'clock.*

   ألـ ______ العاشِرة تماماً.

   as-______ al-xaashira tamaaman.

3. *It's ten past two.*

الساعة ______ وَعَشر دقائق.

as- saaxa ______ wa xashar daqaa'iq.

4. *It's ten to two.*

الساعة الثانية إلاّ ______ دقائق.

as- saaxa ath-thaaniya 'illaa ______ daqaa'iq.

5. *It's half past three.*

الساعة الثالِثة و ______.

as- saaxa ath-thaalitha wa ______.

6. *It's a quarter past four.*

الساعة الـ ______ وَالرُبع.

as- saaxa ar-______ wa r-rubux.

7. *It's a quarter to four.*

الساعة الرابِعة إلاّ ______.

as- saaxa ar-raabixa 'illa ______.

8. *It's twelve o'clock noon.*

الساعة ______ عَشر ظُهراً.

as- saaxa ______ xashar DHuhran.

9. *It's between two and four o'clock.*

الساعة بين الثانية ______.

as- saaxa bayna ath-thaniya wa ______.

10. *It's approximately four o'clock in the morning.*

الساعة حوالي الرابعة ________________ .

as- saaxa Hawalii ar-raabixa ________________.

11. *It's eight in the evening.*

الساعة الثامِنة ________________ .

as- saaxa ath-thaamina ________________.

ANSWER KEY

1. الساعة as-saaxa; 2. ساعة saaxa; 3. الثانية ath-thaaniya; 4. عَشَر xashar; 5.النِصف n-niSf; 6. رابِعة raabixa; 7. رُبع rubx; 8. الثانية ath-thaaniyata; 9. الرابِعة r-raabixa; 10. صَباحاً SabaaHan; 11. مساءً masaa'an.

Bring It All Together

Track: Lesson 9 Bring It All Together (Track 3) CD: 3

Now let's bring it all together, and add a little bit more vocabulary and structure.

مَرحباً بِك في شَرِكَتنا	marHaban bik fii sharikatinaa!	*Welcome to our company!*
شُكراً! هَل تأخَّرت؟	shukran! hal ta'akhkhart?	*Thank you! Am I late?*
لا بأس. دعني آخُذُك إلى مَكتَبِك.	laa ba's. daxnii 'aakhudhuka 'ilaa maktabik.	*No problem. Let me take you to your desk.*
يَبدو أنَّ الجَميع مَشغولون جِدّاً!	yabduu 'anna l-jamiix mashghuluun jiddan!	*Everybody looks so busy!*

إنَّه مَكْتَب كَبير! هذا هو حاسوبك وَبإمكانِك أن تَستَعمِل هذا الهاتِف.	'innahu maktab kabiir! haadhaa huwa Haasubuka wa bi 'imkaanika 'an tastaxmil haadhaa l-haatif.	*It's a big office! This is your computer, and you can use this telephone.*
شُكراً! إنني أتَطَلَّع إلى مُقابَلة زُمَلائي.	shukran! 'innanii 'ataTallax 'ilaa muqaabalat zumalaa'ii.	*Thank you! I look forward to meeting my colleagues.*
سأقَدِّمُك لِلجَميع اليَوم بَعْد الظُهر في الإجْتِماع.	sa 'uqaddimuka lil jamiix al-yawm baxd aDH-DHuhr fi l-'ijtimaax.	*I will introduce you to everyone at the meeting this afternoon.*

Work Out 2

How would you say the following times in Arabic?

1. *1:00 pm* ____________________
2. *3:30 am* ____________________
3. *6:00 am* ____________________
4. *8:15 pm* ____________________

ANSWER KEY

1. الساعة الواحِدة مساءً. as-saaxa al-waaHida masaa'an. 2. الساعة الثالِثة وَالنِصف صَباحاً. as-saaxa th-thaalitha wa n-niSf SabaaHan. 3. الساعة السادِسة صَباحاً. as-saaxa s-saadisa SabaaHan. 4. الساعة الثامِنة وَالرُبع مساءً. as-saaxa th-thaamina wa r-rubx masaa'an.

Drive It Home

Let's practice ordinal numbers and telling the time once more. Give each hour on the hour, starting with 1:00.

الساعة الواحِدة as-saaxa l-waaHida, الثانية th-thaaniya, الثالِثة th-thaalitha, الرابِعة r-raabixa, الخامِسة al-khaamisa, السادِسة s-saadisa, السابِعة s-saabixa, الثامِنة th-thaamina, التاسِعة t-taasixa, العاشِرة al-xaashira, الحادية عَشرة al-Haadiyata xashra, الثانية عَشرة th-thaaniyyata xashra

Now, add وَالنِصف wa n-niSf to express *half past* the hour.

Finally, add وَالرُبع wa r-rubx to express *quarter past* the hour.

Take It Further: Arabic Script

Turn back to your script guide to practice writing the letters you learned earlier in the lesson. Go to Part 2: Writing Arabic, and complete:

- Group 11: ه and ة

Parting Words

مَبْروك mabruuk! *Congratulations!* You've finished Lesson 9, which means that you know:

- ☐ the names of the days of the week. (Still unsure? Go back to 183.)
- ☐ how to use them along with other time expressions. (Still unsure? Go back to 185.)

- ☐ how to ask what time it is. (Still unsure? Go back to 187.)
- ☐ important vocabulary related to time and routines. (Still unsure? Go back to 188.)
- ☐ how to use it all in a conversation related to the workplace. (Still unsure? Go back to 193.)

Don't forget to practice and reinforce what you've learned by visiting **www.livinglanguage.com/languagelab** for flashcards, games, and quizzes.

Take It Further

Track: Lesson 9 Take It Further (Track 4) CD: 3

Of course, you might also need to ask other questions using the question word كَم kam (*how much, how many*), such as:

كَم السِعر؟	kam as-sixr?	*What's the price?*
كَم الوَزْن؟	kam al-wazn?	*What's the weight?*
كَم دَرَجة الحَرارة؟	kam darajat al-Haraara?	*What is the temperature?*

By the way, remember that the metric system is used in most Arab countries, so you also need to know such words as كيلو kiiluu (*kilogram*), غرام gram (*gram*), سَنتيمِتر santiimitr (*centimeter*), and مِتر mitr (*meter*), as well as the degrees in Celsius rather than in Fahrenheit.

Word Recall

Use the words from the list to complete the sentences below. Then translate your answers into English when you are done.

a. شَهيّ shahiyy; b. الصَيْف aS-Sayf; c. المقهى. al-maqhaa; d. قَريب qariib;
e. الصباح aS-SabaaH; f. الساعة as-saaxa; g. أمام 'amaam; h. حَليب Haliib

1. أتناول الفطور في ________________

'atanaawal al-fuTuur fii ________________.

2. أحب الشاي بالـ________________.

'uHiibu sh-shaay bi l-________________.

3. الجو في ________________ دافئ.

al-jaww fi ________________ daafi'.

4. مَكتب البَريد ________________ المَدرسة.

maktab al-bariid ________________ al-madrasa.

5. هل هذا العنوان ________________؟

hal haadha l-xunwaan ________________?

6. الغداء ________________.

al-ghadaa' ________________.

7. نتناول القهوة في ________________

natanaawal al-qahwa fii ________________

8. ________________ الرابعة بعد الظهر.

________________ r-raabixa baxd aDH-DHuhr.

ANSWER KEY

1. e (*I have breakfast in the morning.*) 2. h (*I like tea with milk.*) 3. b (*The weather in the summer is warm.*) 4. g (*The post office is in front of the school.*) 5. d (*Is this address close/near?*) 6. a (*Lunch is delicious.*) 7. c (*We have coffee in the café.*) 8. f (*The time is 4:00 pm.*)

Now match each English phrase or sentence with its Arabic equivalent

1. *I want meat and chicken.*	a. كَم دَرَجة الحرارة؟ **kam darajat al-Haraara?**
2. *We drink coffee.*	b. الساعة الثانية إلاّ عَشر دقائق. **as-saaxa th-thaaniya 'illaa xashr daqaa'iq.**
3. *I like Saturday and Sunday.*	c. الساعة العاشِرة صباحاً. **as-saaxa l-xaashira SabaaHan.**
4. *It's 10:00 am.*	d. أَتَطَلَّع إلى مقابلَة زُمَلائي. **'ataTallax 'ilaa muqaabalat zumalaa'ii.**
5. *I look forward to meeting my colleagues.*	e. أريد لَحم وَدجاج. **'uriidu laHm wa dajaaj.**
6. *What is the temperature?*	f. يذهبون إلى المدرسة كل يوم. **yadhhabuun 'ilaa l-madrasa kulla yawm.**
7. *It's ten to two.*	g. نَشرَب القَهوة. **nashrabu l-qahwa.**
8. *They go to school every day.*	h. أُحب يوم السبت وَيوم الأحد. **'uHibbu yawm as-sabt wa yawm al-'aHad.**

ANSWER KEY

1. e; 2. g; 3. h; 4. c; 5. d; 6. a; 7. b; 8. f

Lesson 10: Entertainment

ألدَرس ألعاشِر: الترفيه

ad-dars al-xashiir: at-tarfiih

مَرحباً! marhaban! *Welcome!* We are almost at the end of our course, and for this last bit, we should have some fun. Let's go to the beach! While you're there, you'll learn:

- □ key vocabulary for nature, including the beach
- □ some more plural forms of nouns
- □ key vocabulary for talking about sports and recreation
- □ how to form the comparative (*bigger*) and superlative (*biggest*)
- □ how to bring it all together in a short conversation about planning your free time

So, are you ready for your last lesson of *Essential Arabic*? هيّا نَبدَأ haya nabda'a! *Let's begin!*

Vocabulary Builder 1

Track: Lesson 10 Vocabulary Builder 1 (Track 5) CD: 3

I love	أُحِبّ	'uHibb
sea	بَحْر	baHr
boat	مَرْكِب	markib

shore, beach	شاطِئ	shaaTi'
sand	رَمل	raml
swimming	السِباحة	as-sibaaHa
running	الجَري	al-jariy
mountains	جِبال	jibaal
lake	بُحَيرة	buHayra
river	نَهر	nahr
forest	غابة	ghaaba
desert	صَحراء	SaHraa'

Vocabulary Practice 1

Translate the following into Arabic:

1. *swimming* ___
2. *lake* ___
3. *forest* ___
4. *beach* ___
5. *sand* ___
6. *desert* ___

ANSWER KEY

1. السِباحة as-sibaaHa; 2. بُحَيرة buHayra; 3. غابة ghaaba; 4. شاطِئ shaaTi'; 5. رَمل raml; 6. صَحراء SaHraa'

Grammar Builder 1

Track: Lesson 10 Grammar Builder 1 (Track 6) CD: 3

MORE ON PLURALS

Back in Lesson 2, you learned that most Arabic nouns form their plurals not by adding an ending, but rather by changing their vowel pattern. Take a look at these examples:

SINGULAR	PLURAL
بَحْر baHr (*sea*)	بِحار biHaar (*seas*)
رَمل raml (*sand*)	رِمال rimaal (*sands*)
نَهر nahr (*river*)	أنهار 'anhaar (*rivers*)
جَبَل jabal (*mountain*)	جِبال jibaal (*mountains*)

As you can see, in all three examples the same basic root consonants are used in both the singular and plural: ب-ح-ر b-H-r for *sea/s*, ر-م-ل r-m-l for *sand/s*, ج-ب-ل j-b-l for *mountain/s*. Do you remember that the Arabic verbs you first learned in Lesson 4 are made up of three root consonants? Most nouns are the same. Think of the three root consonants as the skeleton of a word, and you can manipulate the word—for instance form the plural of a noun or conjugate a verb—by changing the pattern of vowels that hang on that skeleton.

There are common patterns of vowels that nouns use in the plural; for instance, you can see that بِحار biHaar (*seas*), رِمال rimaal (*sands*), and جِبال jibaal (*mountains*) all use the pattern CiCaaC in the plural, where C represents any consonant. Plurals are not generally predictable, so you've just got to memorize each one.

Note, though, that some plurals are regular, formed by simply adding an ending. For example, a lot of feminine nouns that end in ة a take the plural ending ات -aat.

SINGULAR	PLURAL
بُحَيرة buHayra *(lake)*	بُحيرات buHayraat *(lakes)*
غابة ghaaba *(forest)*	غابات ghaabaat *(forests)*

Inanimate singulars that are longer and more complex than typical Arabic nouns with three root consonants also take the plural ending ات -aat.

SINGULAR	PLURAL
تِليفزيون tilifizyuun *(television)*	تِليفزيونات tilifizyuunaat *(televisions)*
كُمبيوتَر kuumbyuutar *(computer)*	كُمبيوتَرات kuumbyuutaraat *(computers)*

And a lot of masculine nouns, including nationalities and many professions, take the plural ending ون -uun.

SINGULAR	PLURAL
مُدرِّس mudarris *(teacher)*	مُدَرِّسون mudarrisuun *(teachers)*
مِصريّ miSrii *(Egyptian)*	مِصريون miSriyuun *(Egyptians)*

Take It Further: Arabic Script

In this last lesson of Essential Arabic, let's complete your knowledge of the Arabic alphabet with hamza and some other special written symbols. Turn to Part 1: Reading Arabic, and read:

- Group 12: shadda, laam-'alif, and the definite article
- 13: hamza
- 14: 'alif maqSuura
- 15: Grammatical endings with -n
- 16: Other symbols

Vocabulary Builder 2

Track: Lesson 10 Vocabulary Builder 2 (Track 7) CD: 3

player	لاعِب	laaxib
sports	رِياضة	riyaaDa
team	فَريق	fariiq
skillful	ماهِر	maahir
game	مُباراة	mubaaraa
basketball	كُرة السَلّة	kurat as-salla
ball	كُرة	kura
to win	يَفوز	yafuuz

winner	فائز	faa'iz
better	أفْضَل	'afDal
best	الأفضَل	al-'afDal
worse	أسوَأ	'aswa'
worst	الأسوأ	al-'aswa'

Vocabulary Practice 2

Translate the following words into English. You'll find the transliteration with the answers. See if you can read the words in Arabic script.

1. أسوَأ ____________
2. كُرة ____________
3. فَريق ____________
4. الأفضَل ____________
5. كُرة السَلّة ____________
6. لاعِب ____________

ANSWER KEY

1. 'aswa', *worse*; 2. kura, *ball*; 3. fariiq, *team*; 4. al-'afDal, *best*; 5. kurat as-salla, *basketball* 6. laaxib, *player*

Grammar Builder 2

Track: Lesson 10 Grammar Builder 2 (Track 8) CD: 3

COMPARING THINGS

The comparative (*more, -er*) of an adjective has the form 'aCCaC. In other words, you take the root consonants of the basic adjective, add أ 'a to the beginning, and ´ a between the second and third to form the word. For example:

ADJECTIVE	COMPARATIVE
كَبير kabiir (*big*)	أكبَر 'akbar (*bigger*)
ماهِر maahir (*clever, skillful*)	أمهَر 'amhar (*more clever, more skillful*)

The comparative form can be used as an adverb or as an adjective, followed by the preposition مِن min, which can be translated in this case as *than*.

أُحِبُّ هذا أفضَل.	'uHibbu haadhaa 'afDal.	*I like this better.*
الرياضة أَفضَل مِن النُزهة.	ar-riyaaDa 'afDal min an-nuzha.	*Sports are better than walking.*

The Arabic superlative form is constructed by adding the definite article ال al to the comparative form.

الأفْضَل	al-'afDal	*the best*
الأسوَأ	al-'aswa'	*the worst*

الأَمْهَر	al-'amhar	*the most clever, the most skillful*

Work Out 1

Track: Lesson 10 Work Out 1 (Track 9) CD: 3

Listen to your audio, and then fill in the missing words that you hear in the sentences listed below:

1. *I love the sea.*

   ________ البَحر.

   al-baHr.

2. *I love swimming in the sea.*

   أُحِبُّ السِباحة ________.

   'uHibbu as-sibaaHa ________.

3. *I also love swimming in the lake.*

   أحب أيضاً السباحة ________.

   'uHibbu 'ayDan as-sibaaHa ________.

4. *But swimming in the river is better.*

   وَلكن السباحة في النهر ________.

   wa lakin as-sibaaHa fi l-nahr ________.

5. *I also love the desert and the forest.*

أُحِبّ أيضاً ________ وَالغابة.

'uHibbu 'ayDan ________ wa l-ghaaba.

6. *But the sea is the best!*

وَلكن البَحر هو ________.

wa lakin al-baHr huwa ________!

ANSWER KEY

1. أُحِبُّ 'uHibbu; 2. في البَحر fi l-baHr; 3. في البُحَيرة fi l-buHayra; 4. أَفضَل 'afDal; 5. الصَحراء aS-SaHraa'; 6. الأفضَل al-'afDal

Bring It All Together

Track: Lesson 10 Bring It All Together (Track 10) CD: 3

Now let's bring it all together and add a little bit more vocabulary and structure.

أقضي اليَوم على شاطِئ البَحر مَعَ أصدِقائي.	'aqDii al-yawm xala shaati' al-baHr maxa 'aSdiqaa'ii.	*I am spending the day at the beach with my friends.*
نحن نُحِبّ السِباحة في البَحر.	naHnu nuHibb as-sibaaHa fi l-baHr.	*We love swimming in the sea.*
و النُزهة على شاطِئ البَحر.	wa n-nuzha xala shaaTi' al-baHr.	*And walking on the seashore.*

بَعد الظُهر سَنَلْعَب مُباراة رياضيّة.	baxd aDH-DHuhr sanalxab mubaaraa riyaaDiyya.	*In the afternoon, we'll play a game of sports.*
رُبَّما مُباراة كُرة السَلّة.	rubbamaa mubaaraat kurat as-salla.	*Maybe a game of basketball.*
فَريق أحْمَد ماهِر جِداً.	fariiq 'aHmad maahir jiddan.	*Ahmad's team is very skillful.*
لكِن فَريقي أفضَل.	laakin fariiqii 'afDal.	*But my team is better.*
لَقَد فُزنا.	laqad fuznaa!	*We won!*
إنَّه يَوم عَظيم.	innahu yawm xaDHiim!	*What a great day!*

Take It Further

Now let's go over some of the new vocabulary you've just heard. أقضي 'aqDii means *I spend time doing something.* سَنلعب sa nalxab is the future tense of the verb يَلعَب yalxab (*to play*), meaning *we'll play*; فُزنا fuznaa is the past tense of the verb يَفوز yafuuz (*to win*), meaning *we won*. And أصدِقائي 'aSdiqaa'ii is the irregular plural of the masculine word صَديق Sadiiq (*friend*) along with the suffix meaning *my*. Can you guess what the feminine form of the word *friend* is? Yes, it's صَديقة Sadiiqa.

Work Out 2

Let's practice the comparative form of adjectives. You'll see an adjective, followed by two subjects. Form a comparative sentence and then translate, following this example:

طَويل Tawiil (*tall*), الوَلَد al-walad, البِنت al-bint
الوَلَد أَطوَل مِن البِنت al-walad 'aTwal min al-bint. (*The boy is taller than the girl.*)

1. كَبير kabiir (*big*), البِنت al-bint, الوَلَد al-walad __________
2. قَريب qariib (*near*), المَكْتَب al-maktab, السوق as-suuq __________
3. جَميل jamiil (*pretty*), الشاطِئ ash-shaaTi', المَدينة al-madiina __________
4. صَغير Saghiir (*small*), المَدرسة al-madrasa, الجامِعة al-jaamixa __________
5. قصير qaSiir (*short*), الفيلم al-film, الكِتاب al-kitaab __________
6. قَديم qadiim (*old*), الهاتِف al-haatif, الحاسوب al-Haasuub __________

ANSWER KEY

1. البِنت أكبَر مِن الوَلَد. al-bint 'akbar min al-walad. (*The girl is bigger than the boy.*)
2. المَكتَب أقرَب مِن السوق. al-maktab 'aqrab min as-suuq. (*The office is nearer than the market.*)
3. الشاطِئ أجمَل مِن المَدينة. ash-shaaTi' 'ajmal min al-madiina. (*The beach is prettier than the city.*)
4. المَدرَسة أصغَر مِن الجامِعة. al-madrasa 'aSghar min al-jaamixa. (*The school is smaller than the university.*)
5. الفيلم أقصَر مِن الكِتاب. al-film 'aqSar min al-kitaab. (*The film is shorter than the movie.*)
6. الهاتِف أقدَم مِن الحاسوب. al-haatif 'aqdam min al-Haasuub. (*The telephone is older than the computer.*)

Drive It Home

Let's practice the verb أُحِبُّ 'uHibbu (*I like*) along with things that you may enjoy. Form full sentences with the following places and activities:

البَحر al-baHr, الشاطِئ ash-shaaTi', السِباحة as-sibaaHa, الجَري al-jariy, الجِبال al-jibaal, البُحَيرات al-buHayraat, الصَحراء as-saHraa', كُرَة السَلّة kurat as-salla, الرياضة ar-riyaaDa

Do you remember what all of that means? That's: *the sea, the beach, swimming, running, the mountains, lakes, the desert, basketball, sports.* That wasn't very hard, was it? Let's throw in a few more forms. Instead of أُحِبُّ 'uHibbu (*I like*), use the following verbs:

أنتَ تُحِبُّ 'anta tuHibbu (*you [m.] like*)

أنتِ تُحِبّينَ 'anti tuHibbiina (*you [f.] like*)

هوَ يُحِبُّ huwa yuHibbu (*he likes*)

هيَ تُحِبُّ hiya tuHibbu (*she likes*)

نَحنُ نُحِبُّ naHnu nuHibbu (*we like*)

Take It Further: Arabic Script

Turn back to your script guide to practice writing the letters you learned earlier in the lesson. Go to Part 2: Writing Arabic, and complete:

- Group 12: shadda, laam-'alif, and the definite article
- 13: hamza
- 14: 'alif maqSuura and grammatical endings with -n.

Parting Words

مَبروك **mabruuk!** *Congratulations!* You've just finished the last lesson of *Essential Arabic*. That means that you now know:

- ☐ key vocabulary for nature, including the beach. (Still unsure? Go back to 199.)
- ☐ some more plural forms of nouns. (Still unsure? Go back to 201.)
- ☐ key vocabulary for talking about sports and recreation. (Still unsure? Go back to 203.)
- ☐ how to form the comparative (*bigger*) and superlative (*biggest*). (Still unsure? Go back to 205.)
- ☐ how to bring it all together in a short conversation about planning some free time. (Still unsure? Go back to 207.)

Don't forget to practice and reinforce what you've learned by visiting **www.livinglanguage.com/languagelab** for flashcards, games, and quizzes.

Now you can test yourself and practice what you've learned with the final Word Recall and quiz, followed by five conversational dialogues that will bring together the Arabic you've seen so far. Until then, حظاً سَعيداً **HaDHan saxiidan!** *Best of luck!*

Word Recall

Choose the most logical selection to make a phrase or sentence, and then translate into English.

1. أَلعَبُ 'alxabu
   a. كُرة السَلّة kurat as-salla
   b. صَغير Saghiir
   c. شَهر shahr
2. الفريق al-fariiq
   a. نُحِبُّ nuHibbu
   b. مَكْتَب البَريد maktab al-bariid
   c. ماهر maahir
3. الساعة as-saaxa
   a. خامِس khaamis
   b. الثانية ath-thaaniya
   c. غُرْفَة طَعام ghurfat Taxaam
4. أذهب إلى المَدرسة 'adhhabu 'ilaa l-madrasa
   a. شارِع shaarix
   b. طَويلات Tawiilaat
   c. كلَّ يَوْم kulla yawm
5. نَتَناوَلُ الفُطور natanaawalu al-fuTuur
   a. بالليل bi l-layl
   b. بقالة biqaala
   c. في الصباح fi S-SabaaH
6. دَرَجة الحرارة في الخَريف darajat al-Haraara fi l-khariif
   a. سُكَّر sukkar
   b. مُعْتَدِلة muxtadila
   c. دافئ daafi'
7. يأكُلُ ya'kulu
   a. عُنوان xunwaan
   b. دجاج dajaaj
   c. سَعيد saxiid

8. في مَكتبي هناك
fii maktabii hunaaka

a. شَهيّ shahiyy
b. هاتِف وَحاسوب haatif wa Haasuub
c. طِوال Tiwaal

9. السِباحة as-sibaaHa

a. الفُنْدُق al-funduq
b. رياضة جميلة riyaaDa jamiila
c. زَرقاء zarqaa'

10. الأخبار al-'akhbaar

a. قَمَر qamar
b. جَميل jamiil
c. في الجَريدة fi l-jariida

ANSWER KEY

1. a (*I play basketball.*) 2. c (*The team is skillful.*) 3. b (*It's 2 o'clock.*) 4. c (*I go to school every day.*) 5. c (*We have breakfast in the morning.*) 6. b (*The temperature in the Fall is moderate.*) 7. b (*He eats chicken.*) 8. b (*In my office there is a phone and a computer.*) 9. b (*Swimming is a beautiful sport.*) 10. c (*The news is in the newspaper.*)

Quiz 2

الإمتحان الثاني

al-'imtiHaan ath-thaanii

You've completed all ten lessons! مُمتاز **mumtaaz!** (*Excellent!*) Now let's review. In this section, you'll find a final quiz testing what you learned in Lessons 1–10. We'll make this quiz a bit more challenging by leaving out the phonetic transcription! By now, you should be familiar enough with the Arabic script. Once you've completed the quiz, score yourself to see how well you've done. If you find that you need to go back and review, please do so before continuing on to the final section with review dialogues and comprehension questions.

A. Match the Arabic on the left to the correct English translations on the right.

1. بِقالة	a. *post office*
2. مَطار	b. *university*
3. جامِعة	c. *hotel*
4. فُندُق	d. *airport*
5. مَكْتَب البَريد	e. *supermarket*

B. Fill in the blanks.

1. *What time is it?*

كَم __________________ ؟

2. *It's ten o'clock.*

__________________ العاشِرة.

3. *It's half past three.*

الساعة الثالِثة و __________________ .

4. *It's a quarter past four.*

الساعة الـ __________________ وَالرُبع.

5. *It's ten past two.*

الساعة الـ __________________ وَعَشَر دقائق.

C. Give the correct form of the adjective in parentheses:

1. عائلة __________________ *(big)*

2. صيدلية __________________ *(new)*

3. شِتاء __________________ *(cold)*

4. بيْت __________________ *(close/nearby)*

5. دجاج __________________ *(delicious)*

D. Conjugate the verbs in parentheses into the correct form, then translate each sentence into English:

1. *(love)* نَحْنُ ______ السِباحة في البَحْر.
2. *(eat a meal)* هم ______ العشاء في المَطعَم.
3. *(go)* أنتم ______ إلى السينما.
4. *(drink)* أنتُنَّ ______ القهوة في المقهى دائماً.
5. *(sleep)* أنتِ ______ في غرفة النوم.

E. Translate the following into Arabic:

1. *Miriam is drinking tea, and Ahmad is drinking coffee.*

______

2. *Mustafa and his wife are eating breakfast.*

______

3. *I am eating at the restaurant.*

______

4. *Are the two of them sitting at the café?*

______

5. *Ahmad wants the dessert.*

______

ANSWER KEY

A. 1. e; 2. d; 3. b; 4. c; 5. a

B. 1. الساعة; 2. الساعة; 3. النِصف; 4. الرابِعة; 5. الثانية

C. 1. كَبيرة; 2. جَديدة; 3. بارِد; 4. قَريب; 5. شَهيّ

D. 1. نُحِبُ; 2. يَتَناولون; 3. تَذهَبون; 4. تَشْرَبْنَ; 5. تَنامين

E. 1. مَريم تشرب شاي وَأحمد يشرب قهوة. 2. مُصطفى وَزوجته يأكلان الفُطور. 3. آكُلُ في المَطْعَم. 4. هَل يجْلِسان في المَقهى؟ 5. أَحْمَد يُريد الحلو.

How Did You Do?

Give yourself a point for every correct answer, then use the following key to determine whether or not you're ready to move on:

0–10 points: It's probably best to go back and study the lessons again to make sure you understood everything completely. Take your time; it's not a race! Make sure you spend time reviewing the vocabulary and reading through each Grammar Builder section carefully.

11–18 points: If the questions you missed were in sections A or B, you may want to review the vocabulary from previous lessons again; if you missed answers mostly in sections C, D, or E check the Grammar Builder sections to make sure you have your grammar basics down.

19–25 points: Feel free to move on to the Review Dialogues! Great job!

points

Review Dialogues

مَرْحباً **marhaban!** *Welcome!* Here's your chance to practice all the vocabulary and grammar you've mastered in ten lessons of *Living Language Essential Arabic* with these five everyday dialogues. The dialogues contain some new material as well, which is meant to give you practice figuring out meaning from context. But of course, the translations are provided as well in case you get stuck. These dialogues are also an opportunity to practice reading Arabic script. You'll see each dialogue first in Arabic, followed by the translation. The phonetic transliteration is given last, so try to read the Arabic script on its own. Reading along as you listen to the audio will help you develop stronger reading skills.

Each dialogue is followed by comprehension questions, so you'll be able to test yourself on how well you've understood the dialogue. And to practice your pronunciation, don't forget to repeat along after the audio. As always, look for ▶. You'll hear the dialogue in Arabic first, then in Arabic and English. Next, for practice, you'll do some role play by taking part in the conversation yourself!

وَقتاً سَعيداً **waqtan saxiidan** *Have fun!*

Dialogue 1

بيت أحْمَد الجَديد

bayt 'aHmad al-jadiid

AHMAD'S NEW HOUSE

Arabic Only – Track: 11 CD: 3 English and Arabic – Track: 12 CD: 3 Role Play Exercise – Track: 13 CD: 3

أهلاً يا نَبيلة!

أهلاً يا أحْمَد! كيْف الحال؟

بِخَير – شُكراً. أهلاً بِكِ في بَيتي الجَديد!

إنَّهُ بيت كَبير! وَمُشْمِس أيضاً!

نَعَم – نَحنُ سُعَداء جِداً هُنا. لَدَينا غُرفة جُلوس كَبيرة وَثلاث غُرَف نَوم وَحَديقة جَميلة.

وَهَل فَعَلْتَ كُلَّ هذِه التَجديدات؟

كَلاّ – المَطْبَخ وَالحمّام كانا جديدين.

أُنظُر إلى هذه الشُرَف الكَبيرة في غُرفة الطَعام! بالتأكيد هذه الغُرفة دافئة دائماً في الصباح.

نَعَم زَوجَتي وَالأولاد يُحِبون تناول الفطور هنا في الصَباح.

وَهَل هذا الأثاث جَديد؟

كَلاّ إنّه مِن بَيتِنا القَديم وَلكِن أثاث غُرفة المَكْتَب جَديد.

هَل البيت قريب من مَكتَبِكَ؟

نَعَم. وَأيضاً قَريب مِن مَكتَب زَوجَتي وَمَدْرَسة الأولاد.

عَظيم! وَأيضاً قَريب مِن بَيت أخيك، أليس كَذلِك؟

نَعَم، أخي وَعائلَته يَسكُنون بِجانِب مَيدان الثَورة. إنّها نُزهة قَريبة من هُنا.

مَبروك يا أَحْمَد! إنّه بيت جَميل.

شُكراً. إنّنا مَحظوظون جِداً.

Hello, Nabila!

Hello, Ahmad! How are you?

I'm well, thank you. Welcome to my new house!

This is a big house! And sunny too!

Yes, we're very happy here. We have a big living room, three bedrooms, and a beautiful garden.

And did you make all these renovations?

No, the kitchen and the bathroom were new.

Look at these big windows in the dining room! This room must always be very warm in the morning.

Yes, my wife and children love to have breakfast here in the morning.

And is this furniture new?

No, it's from our old house. But the furniture in the study is new.

Is the house near your office?

Yes, and also near my wife's office and the children's school.

Wonderful! And also near your brother's house, right?

Yes, my brother and his family live near Al-Thawra Square; it's a short walk from here.

Congratulations, Ahmad! It's a beautiful house.

Thank you. We're very lucky.

'ahlan, ya nabiila!

'ahlan, yaa 'aHmad! kayf al-Haal?

bi khayr - shukran. 'ahlan biki fii baytii al-jadiid!

'innahu bayt kabiir! wa mushmis 'ayDan!

naxam, naHnu suxadaa' jiddan hunaa. ladaynaa ghurfat juluus kabiira wa thalaath ghuraf nawm wa Hadiiqa jamiila.

wa hal faxalta kulla haadhihi t-tajdiidaat?

kallaa, al-maTbakh wa l-Hammaam kaanaa jadiidayn.
'unDHur 'ilaa haadhihi ash-shuraf al-kabiira fii ghurfat aT-Taxaam! bi t-ta'akiid hadhihi al-ghurfa daafi'a daa'iman fi S-SabaaH.
naxam. zawjatii wa l-'awlaad yuHibbuun tanaawul al-fuTuur hunaa fi S-SabaaH.
wa hal haadhaa l-'athaath jadiid?
kalla, 'innahu min baytinaa al-qadiim. wa laakin 'athaath ghurfat al-maktab jadiid.
hal al-bayt qariib min maktabika?
naxam. wa 'ayDan qariib min maktab zawjatii wa madrasat al-'awlaad.
xaDHiim! wa 'ayDan qariib min bayt akhiik, 'alaysa kadhaalik?
naxam, 'akhii wa xaa'ilatuhu yaskunuun bijaanib maydaan ath-thawra; 'innahaa nuzha qariiba min hunaa.
mabruuk, yaa aHmad! 'innahu bayt jamiil.
shukran. 'innana maHDHuuDHuun jiddan.

Dialogue 1 Practice

Answer the following comprehension questions about Dialogue 1. Again, the transliteration appears separately, after the script, so use this as an opportunity to continue to build your reading skills in Arabic.

1. مِن عنده بيت جديد؟ أَحمَد أو نَبيلة؟ ______
2. هَل البيت كبير أو صَغير؟ ______
3. هل البَيت مُشمِس؟ ______
4. أيّ غُرَف جَديدة؟ ______
5. هل البيت قريب مِن مَدْرَسة الأولاد؟ ______
6. أيْنَ يَسْكنُ أخو أحْمَد؟ ______

1. man xindahu bayt jadiid? 'ahmad 'aw nabiila? ______________________

2. hal al-bayt kabiir 'aw Saghiir? ______________________

3. hal al-bayt mushmis? ______________________

4. 'ayya ghuraf jadiida? ______________________

5. hal al-bayt qariib min madrasat al-'awlaad? ______________________

6. 'ayna yaskunu 'akhuu 'aHmad? ______________________

ANSWER KEY:

1. أحْمَد 'aHmad, *Ahmad*; 2. كَبير kabiir, *big*; 3. نَعم naxam, *yes*; 4. المَطْبَخ وَالحَمام al-maTbakh wa l-Hamaam, *the kitchen and bathroom*; 5. نَعم naxam, *yes*; 6. قريب qariib, *close by*, بِجانِب مَيدان الثورة bijaanib maydaan ath-thawra, *near Al-Thawra Square*

Dialogue 2

'aHmad wa muna yatanawalaan al-xashaa'

أحْمَد وَمُنى يَتَناوَلان العَشاء

AHMAD AND MONA HAVE DINNER

Arabic Only - Track: 14 CD: 3 English and Arabic - Track: 15 CD: 3 Role Play Exercise - Track: 16 CD: 3

هذا مَطْعَم لَطيف يا أَحمَد.

نَعَم يا مُنى إنَّهُ جَيِّد جَدّاً لِلعَشاء.

هُناكَ مأكولات شهية كثيرة في قائمة الطَعام.

أنا أُريد شوربة الخُضروات.

أو رُبّما شوربة العَدْس؟

مُمكِن أن نطْلُب شوربَتين مُخْتَلِفَتين.

وَبعْد الشوربة أُريدُ سَلَطة شَهيّة؟

فِكْرة هائلة! السَلَطة جيدة جداً في الصيف.

وَأَنْتَ ماذا تُريد؟

سأتَناوَل الدَجاج المَشوي مَع الأرُز.

إختيار جَيِّد جِدّاً.

وَهيّا نَطْلُب كوبيّ ماء.

بِالتأكيد - وَبَعْض الخُبْز.

الخُبز هُنا دائماً طازَج.

وَبَعْد العَشاء مُمكِن أن نَطْلُب الحُلو.

أُريد بَعض البقلاوة وَفُنجان قَهوة.

أريد فُنجان قَهوة أيضاً. سَنَطْلُبُ فُنجانيّ قَهوة.

بالتأكيد.

وَفيما بَعْد مُمكِن أنْ نَذْهَب إلى السينِما.

عَظيم هَيا نَطْلُب.

This is a nice restaurant, Ahmad.
Yes, Mona. It's very good for dinner.
There are a lot of delicious things on the menu.
I'd like a vegetable soup.
Or maybe the lentil soup?
We can order two different soups.
And after the soup, I'd like a delicious salad.
Great idea! Salad's very good in the summer.
And you, what would you like?

I'll have the grilled chicken with rice.
A very good choice!
And let's order two glasses of water.
Of course. And some bread.
The bread here is always fresh.
And after dinner we can order dessert.
I'd like some baklava and a cup of coffee.
I'd like coffee, too. We'll order two cups of coffee.
Certainly.
And later we can go to the cinema.
Wonderful! Let's order!

haadhaa maTxam laTiif, yaa 'aHmad.
naxam yaa munaa, 'innahu jayyid jiddan li l-xashaa'.
hunaaka ma'kuulaat shahiyya kathiira fii qaa'imat aT-Taxaam.
'aana 'uriidu shuurbat al-khuDrawaat.
'aw rubbamaa shurbat al-xads?
mumkin 'an naTlub shuurbatayn mukhtalifatayn.
wa baxd ash-shuurba 'uriidu salaTa shahiyya.
fikra haa'ila! as-salaTa jayyida jiddan fi S-Sayf.
wa 'anta, maadha turiid?
sa-'atanaawal ad-dajaaj al-mashwii maxa al-'aruzz.
'ikhtiyaar jayyid jiddan!
wa hayaa naTlub kuubayy maa'.
bi t-ta'kiid. wa baxD al-khubz.
al-khubz hunaa daa'iman Taazaj.
wa baxd al-xashaa' mumkin 'an naTlub al-Hulw.
'uriidu baxD al-baqlaawa wa funjaan qahwa.
'uriidu funjaan qahwa 'ayDan. sanaTlub funjaanay qahwa.
bi t-ta'kiid.
wa fiimaa baxd mumkin 'an nadhhab 'ilaa s-siinimaa.
xaDHiim! hayyaa naTlub!

Dialogue 2 Practice

1. أينَ أحْمَد وَمُنى؟ ____________________

2. أيَ وَجْبة يتناولان؟ ____________________

3. هل السَلَطة جيِّدة في الصَيْف؟ ____________________

4. كيف الخُبز في المَطْعَم؟ ____________________

5. ماذا يَشرب أحْمَد مَعَ الحُلو؟ ____________________

6. إلى أين يذهب أحمَد وَمُنى بَعد العَشاء؟ ____________________

1. 'ayna 'aHmad wa munaa? ____________________

2. 'ayya wajba yatanaawalaan? ____________________

3. hal as-salaTa jayyida fi S-Sayf? ____________________

4. kayfa al-khubz fii l-maTxam? ____________________

5. maadha yashrab 'aHmad maxa l-Hulw? ____________________

6. 'ilaa 'ayna yadhhab 'aHmad wa munaa baxd al-xashaa'? ____________________

ANSWER KEY

1. في المَطعَم fii l-maTxam, *at the restaurant*; 2. العَشاء al-xashaa', *dinner*; 3. نَعم naxam, *yes*; 4. دائماً طازَج daa'iman Taazaj, *always fresh*; 5. قَهوة qahwa, *coffee*; 6. السينما as-siinimaa, *the movies*

Dialogue 3

fi l-biqaala

في البِقالة

AT THE SUPERMARKET

Arabic Only - Track: 17 CD: 3 English and Arabic - Track: 18 CD: 3 Role Play Exercise - Track: 19 CD: 3

هَل نَحتاج حليب يا مُنى؟

نَعَم يا أحمَد. نَحتاج حليب وَسُكَّر.

حَسَناً. وَما هي الخضروات التي تريدينها؟

بَعض السَلَطة الطازجة وَالطماطم وَالخيار.

رُبَما نستطيع أيضاً أن نشتري بَعض البطاطا وَالفاصوليا الخضراء.

نَعم! وَنحتاج بعض الأرز أيضاً.

وَالشاي.

وَبَعض الحلوى للأولاد.

وَبَعض الفاكهة.

هذا البطيخ شهيّ.

عَظيم! سَنَشتري بَطيخة وَبَعض التفاح الأحمَر.

هَل تَحتاج بَعض الأقلام لِمَكْتَبِكَ؟

نَعم، رُبّما ثلاثة أقلام - قَلَم أزْرَق وَقَلَم أحْمَر وَقَلَم أسْوَد.

وَبَعض الأقلام للأولاد أيضاً. هُنا خَمَسة أقلام زَرقاء.

يَجِبُ أيضاً أن نَشتري هَديّة لأُختي لأن عيد ميلادها الأسبوع القادِم.

مُمكِن أن نشتري لها كِتاب.

نَعم، إنّها سَتَكون سَعيدة بهذا.

المَكْتَبة بِجانِب البِقالة.

هيا نشتري الخُضروات ثُمَّ نَذهّب إلى المَكْتَبة.

عظيم، هيّا بنا.

Mona, do we need milk?
Yes, Ahmad. We need milk and sugar.
All right. And what are the vegetables that you need?
Some fresh salad, tomatoes, and cucumbers.
Maybe we can also buy some potatoes and green beans?
Yes! And we need some rice as well.
And tea.
And some dessert for the children.
And some fruit.
This watermelon looks delicious!
Wonderful! We'll buy a watermelon and some red apples.
Do you need some pens for your office?
Yes, maybe three pens. A blue pen, a red pen, and a black pen.
And some pens for the children, too. Here are five blue pens.
We must also buy a present for my sister because her birthday is next week.
We can buy her a book.
Yes, she'd be happy with that.
The bookstore is next to the supermarket.
Let's buy the vegetables then go to the bookstore.
Great! Let's go.

hal naHtaaj Haliib, ya munaa?
naxam, ya 'aHmad. naHtaaju Haliib wa sukkar.

Hasanan. wa maa hiya al-khudrawaat 'allatii turiidiinahaa?

baxD as-salaTa aT-Taazija wa T- TamaaTim wa l-khiyaar.

rubbamaa nastaTiixu 'ayDan 'an nashtarii baxD al-baTaaTaa wa l-faaSuuliyaa l-khadraa'.

naxam! wa naHtaju baxD al-'aruzz 'ayDan.

wa sh-shaay.

wa baxD al-Halwaa li l-'awlaad.

wa baxD al-faakiha.

haadhaa al-baTiikh shahiyy!

xaDHiim! sa-nashtarii baTiikha wa baxD at-tufaaH al-'aHmar.

hal taHtaaju baxD al-'aqlaam li-maktabika?

naxam, rubbamaa thalaathata 'aqlaam. qalam 'azraq wa qalam 'aHmar wa qalam 'aswad.

wa baxD al-'aqlaam li l-'awlaad 'ayDan. hunaa khamsat 'aqlaam zarqaa'.

yajib 'ayDan 'an nashtarii hadiyya li-'ukhtii li'anna xiid miilaaduhaa l-'usbuux al-qaadim.

mumkin 'an nashtarii lahaa kitaab.

naxam, 'innahaa satakuun saxiida bi haadhaa.

al-maktaba bijaanib al-biqaala.

hayaa nashtarii l-khuDrawaat thumma nadhhab 'ilaa l-maktaba

xaDHiim! hayaa binaa.

Dialogue 3 Practice

1. هَل يحتاج أحمَد وَمُنى حليب؟ ________________

2. هل تريد مُنى الخيار؟ ________________

3. هل يشتري أحمد شاي أو قهوة؟ ________________

4. أي فاكهة يشتريان؟ ________________

5. لِمن الحَلوى؟ ________________

6. لماذا يريد أحمَد هدية لأُختِه؟ ______

1. hal yaHtaaju 'aHmad wa munaa Haliib? ______

2. hal turiidu munaa l-khiyaar? ______

3. hal yashtarii 'aHmad shaay 'aw qahwa? ______

4. 'ayya faakiha yashtariyaan? ______

5. li man al-Halwaa? ______

6. limaadha yuriid 'aHmad hadiyya li 'ukhtihi? ______

ANSWER KEY

1. نَعم naxam, *yes*; 2. نَعم naxam, *yes*; 3. شاي shaay, *tea*; 4. بَطيخ وَتُفّاح baTiikh wa tufaaH, *watermelon and apples*; 5. لِلأولاد li l-'awlaad, *for the children*; 6. عيد ميلادها الأسبوع القادِم xiid miiladihaa l-'usbuux al-qaadim, *Her birthday is next week.*

Dialogue 4

fi l-funduq

في الفُنْدُق

AT THE HOTEL

Arabic Only - Track: 20 CD: 3 English and Arabic - Track: 21 CD: 3 Role Play Exercise - Track: 22 CD: 3

أهلاً يا سَيِّد جوردون. مَرْحَباً بِك في فُنْدُق سفينكس.

شُكْراً! أنا سعيد جِدّاً بِوجودي هُنا.

هَل هَذِه أَوَّل زيارة لَك هُنا؟

نَعَم. هذِه أوّل زيارة لَي إلى مِصر.

إنَّكَ تَتَكَلَّم العَرَبيّة جَيّداً!

أنا طالِب. أدرُس اللغة العَرَبية.

عَظيم! هَل تُريد غُرفة تُطِلُّ على المَيدان أو على الحَديقة؟

غُرفة تُطِلُّ على الحَديقة مِن فَضْلَك.

إختيار جيّد! إنَّها هادئة وَمُشمِسة في الصباح.

وَهَل الغُرفة فيها حَمّام؟

نَعَم.

وَهَل هُناك تكييف؟

نَعَم. هُناكَ تَكيف في كُلّ الغُرَف.

حَسَب النَشرة الجَويّة الأسبوع القادِم حارّ جِدّاً.

الصَيف في القاهِرة دائماً حار.

نَعَم. حار وَجاف.

هذا صَحيح. هذا مُفتاحُكَ.

شُكراً لِمُساعَدتِك.

Hello, Mr. Gordon. Welcome to the Hotel Sphinx.
Thank you! I'm very happy to be here.
Is this your first visit here?
Yes, this is my first trip to Egypt.
You speak Arabic well!
I'm a student. I study the Arabic language.
Wonderful! Would you like a room overlooking the square or the garden?
A room overlooking the garden, please.

Good choice! It's quiet and sunny in the morning.
And does the room have a bathroom?
Yes.
And is there air-conditioning?
Yes, there is air-conditioning in all rooms.
The weather forecast says it will be very hot weather next week.
Summers in Cairo are always hot.
Yes, hot and dry.
This is true. Here is your key.
Thank you for your help.

'ahlan, ya sayyid gordon. marHaban bika fii funduq sfinks.
shukran! 'anaa saxiid jiddan bi wujuudii hunaa.
hal haadhihi 'awwal ziyaara laka hunaa?
naxam. haadhihii 'awwal ziyaara lii 'ilaa miSr.
'innaka tatakallam al-xarabiyya jayyidan!
'anaa Taalib. 'adrusu l-lugha l-xarabiyya.
xaDHiim! hal turiidu ghurfa tuTillu xala l-maydan 'aw xala l-Hadiiqa?
ghurfa tuTillu xala l-Hadiiqa, min faDlik.
'ikhtiyaar jayyid! 'innahaa haadi'a wa mushmisa fi S-SabaaH.
wa hal al-ghurfa fiihaa Hammaam?
naxam.
wa hal hunaaka takyiif?
naxam. hunaaka takyiif fi kull al-ghuraf.
Hasab 'an-nashra al-jawiyya l-'usbuux al-qaadim Haarr jiddan.
aS-Sayf fi l-qaahira daa'iman Haarr.
naxam, Haarr wa jaaff.
haadhaa SaHiiH. haadhaa muftaaHuka.
shukran li musaaxadatika.

Dialogue 4 Practice

1. ما إسم الفُندق؟ ______________________

2. هل هذه أول زيارة لِجوردون في مِصر؟ ______________________

3. هل يَتَكَلَّم جوردون اللغة العَرَبية؟ ______________________

4. هل تُطِّل غُرفة جوردون على المَيدان أو الحَديقة؟ ______________________

5. هَل الغُرفة فيها حَمام؟ ______________________

6. هل الصيف في مِصر بارِد؟ ______________________

1. maa 'ism al-funduq? ______________________

2. hal haadhihi 'awwal ziyaara li gordon fii miSr? ______________________

3. hal yatakallam gordon al-lugha l-xarabiyya? ______________________

4. hal tuTillu ghurfat gordon xalaa l-maydaan 'aw al-Hadiiqa? ______________________

5. hal al-ghurfa fiihaa Hamaam? ______________________

6. hal aS-Sayf fii miSr baarid? ______________________

ANSWER KEY:

1. سفينكس sfiinks, *Sphinx*; 2. نَعم naxam, *yes*; 3. نَعم naxam, *yes*; 4. الحَديقة al-Hadiiqa, *the garden*; 5. نَعم naxam, *yes*; 6.كلا kallaa, *no*

Dialogue 5

الذَهاب إلى السوق

adh-dhihaab 'ila s-suuq

GOING TO THE SUQ

Arabic Only – Track: 23 CD: 3 English and Arabic – Track: 24 CD: 3 Role Play Exercise – Track: 25 CD: 3

عَفواً، مُمكِن أن تُرشِدَني إلى السوق؟

إستَمرّ في هذا الشارِع حَتى تَصِل إلى المَيدان.

مَيدان الثَورة؟

نَعَم. وَفي مَيدان الثورة إتَّجِه إلى اليَمين وَإسْتَمِر حَتى تَصِل إلى المُسْتَشفى.

هَل المُسْتَشفى قَريب مِن الجامِعة؟

نَعَم، المُستَشفى بِجانِب الجامِعة.

وَالسوق أيضاً بِجانِب الجامِعة؟

السوق خَلْف الجامعة بعد التقاطُع.

هَل هذا بَعيد؟

كلاّ إنّها نُزهة قصيرة مِن هُنا.

لكن اليَوم حار جِدّاً. سأحتاجُ سيارة أُجرة.

هُناكَ سيّارات أُجرة أمام فُندُق النيل.

وَأين فُندُق النيل؟

بِجانِب الصَيدَليّة عَبر الشارِع.

وَمَتى تَفتَح المتاجِر في السوق؟

تَفتَح في الساعة العاشِرة.

رُبّما أتَناوَل فُنجان قَهوة في فُندُق النيل قَبلَ أن أذهَب إلى السوق.

نَعَم لَديكِ ساعة واحِدة قَبلَ إفتِتاح المتاجِر.

شُكراً لِمُساعَدَتِكَ!

بِكُلِّ سُرور! وَقْتاً مُمتِعاً!

Excuse me, can you show me the way to the souk?

Continue on this street till you reach the square.

Al-Thawra Square?

Yes. And at al-Thawra Square you turn right and go straight ahead till you reach the hospital.

Is the hospital near the university?

Yes, the hospital is next to the university.

And is the souk next to the university, too?

The souk is behind the university, after the intersection.

Is it far?

No, it's a short walk from here.

But it's a very hot day. I'll need a taxi.

There are taxis in front of the Nile Hotel.

And where is the Nile Hotel?

It's next to the pharmacy across the street.

At what time do the shops at the souk open?

They open at 10 o'clock.

Maybe I will have a cup of coffee at the Nile Hotel before going to the souk.

Yes, you have one hour before the shops open.

Thank you for your help!

My pleasure! Have a good time!

xafwan, mumkin 'an turshidnii 'ila s-suuq?
'istamirr fii haadhaa sh-shaarix Hattaa taSil 'ila l-maydaan.
maydaan ath-thawra?
naxam. wa fii maydan ath-thawra 'ittajih 'ilaa l-yamiin wa 'istamirr Hattaa taSil 'ila l-mustashafaa.
hal al-mustashfaa qariib min al-jaamixa?
naxam, al-mustashfaa bijaanib al-jaamixa.
wa s-suuq 'ayDan bijaanib aj-jaamixa?
as-suq khalf al-jaamixa, baxd aT-Taqaatux.
hal haadhaa baxiid?
kalla, 'innahaa nuzha qaSiira min hunaa.
laakin al-yawm Haarr jiddan. sa-'aHtaaju sayyaarat 'ujra.
hunaaka sayyaraat 'ujra 'amaam funduq an-niil.
wa 'ayna funduq an-niil?
bijaanib aS-Saydaliyya, xabr ash-shaarix.
wa mataa taftaH al-mataajir fi s-suuq?
tafTah fi s-saaxa l-xaashira.
rubbamaa 'atanaawal funjaan qahwa fi funduq an-niil qabl 'an 'adhhabu 'ila s-suuq.
naxam, ladayka saaxa waaHida qabl 'iftitaaH al-mataajir.
shukran li-musaaxadatika!
bikulli-suruur! waqtan mumtixan!

Dialogue 5 Practice

1. ماذا يُريد الرَجُل؟ ______

2. إلى أين يَتَّجِه عِند مَيدان الثورة؟ ______

3. هل المُستَشفى بِجانِب الجامِعة؟ ______

4. مَتى تَفتَح المتاجِر في السوق؟ ______

5. أينَ سَيّارات الأجرة؟ ____________________

6. ماذا يتناوَل الرَجُل في فُندُق النيل؟ ____________________

1. **maadhaa yuriid ar-rajul?** ____________________

2. **'ilaa 'ayna yattajih xind maydaan ath-thawra?** ____________________

3. **hal al-mustashfaa bijaanib al-jaamixa?** ____________________

4. **mataa taftaH al-mataajir fi s-suuq?** ____________________

5. **'ayna sayyaaraat al-'ujra?** ____________________

6. **maadhaa yatanaawal ar-rajul fii funduq an-niil?** ____________________

ANSWER KEY

1. كيف يَذهَب إلى السوق kayf yadhhab 'ilaa s-suuq, *how to go to the market*; 2. إلى اليمين 'ilaa l-yamiin, *turn right*; 3. نعَم naxam, *yes*; 4. الساعة العاشِرة as-saaxa l-xaashira, *10 o'clock*; 5. أمام فُندُق النيل 'amaama funduq an-niil, *in front of the Nile Hotel*; 6. فُنجان قَهوة funjaan qahwa, *a cup of coffee*

مَبروك mabruuk! *Congratulations!* You've come to the end of *Living Language Essential Arabic*. We hope you've enjoyed your experience and are looking forward to pushing your Arabic studies further along. If you've purchased *Complete* or *Platinum Arabic*, you can now continue on to the second book, *Intermediate Arabic*. Of course, feel free to go back and review at any time, and don't forget to practice online at www.livinglanguage.com/languagelab.

Pronunciation and Transcription Guide

1. VOWELS AND DIPHTHONGS

ـَ	a	*o* in *hot* or *e* in *set*	مَن man (*who*) وَلَـد walad (*boy*)
ـُ	u	*u* in *put* or *oo* in *foot*	هُم hum (*they*) فُنْدُق funduq (*hotel*)
ـِ	i	*i* in *pit*	بِنْت bint (*girl*) إسْم 'ism (*name*)
ا	aa	*o* in *hot* or *e* in *set*, but held longer	كِتاب kitaab (*book*) لا laa (*no*)
ي	ii	*ee* in *seen* (also as a consonant, *y* in *yes*)	كَبير kabiir (*big*) إسْمي 'ismii (*my name*)
و	uu	*oo* in *pool* (also as a consonant, *w* in *want*)	سُرور suruur (*pleasure*) مَبْروك mabruuk (*congratulations*)
ـَوْ	aw	*ou* in *house* or *ow* in *brown.*	يَوم yawm (*day*) زَوْج zawj (*husband*)
ـَيْ	ay	*ai* in *bait* or *y* in *my*	بَيْت bayt (*house*) أينَ 'ayna (*where*)

2. CONSONANTS

ب	b	*b* in *bake* or *bit*	بِنْت **bint** (*girl*) بَيْت **bayt** (*house*)
ت	t	*t* in *take* or *tip*	تَأْكُل **ta'kul** (*she eats*) تَجْلِس **tajlis** (*she sits*)
ث	th	*th* in *thank* or *think* (*not *th* in *this* or *that*)	ثانية **thaaniya** (*second*) ثَلاثة **thalaatha** (*three*)
ج	j	*s* in *measure* or *pleasure*. (In Egypt and Yemen, like the *g* in *go* or *get*. In the eastern Arab world, like the *j* in *jelly* or *joke*.)	جَريدة **jariida** (*newspaper*) جَميل **jamiil** (*pretty*)
ح	H	forceful, constricted *h*, as if blowing on glasses to clean them	حارّ **Haarr** (*hot*) مَسْرَح **masraH** (*theater*)
خ	kh	German *Bach* or Hebrew *Baruch*	أُخْت **'ukht** (*sister*) خَمْسة **khamsa** (*five*)
د	d	*d* in *day* or *do*	دائماً **daa'iman** (*always*) جَريدة **jariida** (*newspaper*)
ذ	dh	*th* in *this*, *that*, or *other*	يَذْهَب **yadhhab** (*he goes*) هَذِه **haadhihi** (*this*)
ر	r	rolled *r* of Italian or Spanish	رِجال **rijaal** (*men*) إِمْرَأة **'imra'a** (*woman*)
ز	z	*z* in *zoo* or *zipper*	زيارة **ziyaara** (*visit*) زَوْج **zawj** (*husband*)

س	s	*s* in *so* or *sit*	سِتَّة sitta (*six*) سَلام salaam (*peace, hello*)
ش	sh	*sh* in *shoe* or *ship*	شُكْراً shukran (*thank you*) شَمْس shams (*sun*)
ص	S	*s* in *set*, but with lowered jaw, from further back in mouth	صَغير Saghiir (*small*) صَديق Sadiiq (*friend*)
ض	D	*d* in *day*, but with lowered jaw, from further back in mouth	أفضَل 'afDal (*better*) أقضي 'aqDii (*I spend*)
ط	T	*t* in *take*, but with lowered jaw, from further back in mouth	طالِبة Taaliba (*student*) طِفْل Tifl (*child*)
ظ	DH	*th* in *this*, but with lowered jaw, from further back in mouth	عَظيم xaDHiim (*great*) ظُهر DHuhr (*noon*)
ع	x	formed with heavy constriction at back of throat, similar to a gagging sound	أَرْبَعة 'arbaxa (*four*) عَشَرَة xashara (*ten*)
غ	gh	similar to the gargled *r* of the French *rue* or *rare*	غداً ghadan (*tomorrow*) غُرْفَة ghurfa (*room*)
ف	f	*f* in *far* or *feel*	في fii (*in*) الفُنْدُق al-funduq (*the hotel*)
ق	q	similar to the sound of a *g* or a *k*, but produced further back in the throat	قَمَر qamar (*moon*) حَديقة Hadiiqa (*garden*)
ك	k	*k* in *kite* or *keep*	كِتاب kitaab (*book*) هُناك hunaak (*there is/are*)

ل	l	*l* in *like* or *let*	لَكِن lakin (*but*) لَطيف laTiif (*friendly, pleasant*)
م	m	*m* in *make* or *meet*	مَكْتَب maktab (*office*) مُمتاز mumtaaz (*wonderful*)
ن	n	*n* in *no* or *night*	أَنا 'anaa (*I*) نَعَم naxam (*yes*)
ه	h	*h* in *here* or *happy*	هَذا haadhaa (*this*) هيَ hiya (*she*)
ء	'	glottal stop, "catch" between syllables in "uh-oh!"	مَساء masaa' (*evening*) عائلة xaa'ila (*family*)
و	w	*w* in *we* or *wool*	طَويل Tawiil (*tall*) الوَلَد al-walad (the *boy*)
ي	y	*y* in *yes* or *yellow*	اليَوم al-yawm (*the day*) يَكْتُب yaktub (*he writes*)

Grammar Summary

1. NOUNS

A. GENDER

Nouns that have natural gender (*man, woman, boy, girl, bull, cow*) have logical grammatical gender. Masculine nouns that denote professions (أُسْتَاذ 'ustaadh, *male professor*) can be made feminine by adding the feminine ending ة -a (أُسْتَاذة 'ustaadha, *female professor*). Inanimate nouns are generally masculine if they end in a consonant, and generally feminine if they end in ة -a. However, there are some irregular inanimate nouns that end in consonants but are feminine, such as شمس shams (*sun*.) Also, nouns denoting parts of the body that exist in pairs (عين xayn, *eye*) are feminine.

B. ARTICLES

The indefinite article is implied in Arabic, so كتاب kitaab can mean *book* or *a book*. The definite article is الـ al, attached to a noun, so الكتاب al-kitaab is *the book*. The ل l in the definite article is assimilated (made the same as the following consonant) before the "sun" consonants ت t-, ث th-, د d-, ذ dh-, ر r-, ز z-, س s-, ش sh-, ص S-, ض D-, ط T-, ظ DH-, and ن n-.

C. PLURALS

Nouns form their plurals in one of two ways. The first type of plural is called a "sound" plural and involves adding an ending to the singular form. Sound plurals are reserved mainly for nouns that denote human profession or nationalities, or inanimate nouns that are too long to follow the system of manipulating root consonants. The human masculine sound plural ending is ون **-uun**, and the human feminine sound plural ending is ـَت **-at** (added to the singular ة **-a** ending to produce ات **-aat**.) Non-human sound plurals have the same ending as the feminine, ات **-aat**.

مُدرِّس **mudarris** *(teacher, m.)*	مُدَرِّسون **mudarrisuun** *(teachers)*
مِصريّ **miSrii** *(Egyptian, m.)*	مِصريون **miSriyuun** *(Egyptians)*
مُدَرِّسَة **mudarrisa** *(teacher, f.)*	مُدَرِّسات **mudarrisaat** *(teachers)*
تِليفزيون **tilifizyuun** *(television)*	تِليفزيونات **tilifizyuunaat** *(televisions)*
كُمبيوتَر **kuumbyuutar** *(computer)*	كُمبيوتَرات **kuumbyuutaraat** *(computers)*
بُحَيرة **buHayra** *(lake)*	بُحيرات **buHayraat** *(lakes)*
غابة **ghaaba** *(forest)*	غابات **ghaabaat** *(forests)*

Most nouns take "broken" plurals, which involve altering the vowels before, after, or between their root consonants. Broken plurals follow general patterns, but they must be memorized. The following are the most common patterns for forming broken plurals. The letter **C** indicates any root consonant.

PATTERN	SINGULAR EXAMPLES	PLURAL EXAMPLES
'aCCaaC	وَلَد walad *(boy)* وَقْت waqt *(time)*	أَوْلَاد 'awlaad *(boys)* أَوْقَات 'awqaat *(times)*
CuCuuC	فَنّ fann *(art)* مَلِك malik *(king)*	فُنُون funuun *(arts)* مُلُوك muluuk *(kings)*
CiCaaC	كَلْب kalb *(dog)* رَجُل rajul *(man)*	كِلَاب kilaab *(dogs)* رِجَال rijaal *(men)*
CuCuC	كِتَاب kitaab *(book)* مَدِينَة madiina *(city)*	كُتُب kutub *(books)* مُدُن mudun *(cities)*
CuCaC	دَوْلَة dawla *(country)* غُرْفَة ghurfa *(room)*	دُوَل duwal *(countries)* غُرَف ghuraf *(rooms)*
'aCCuC	شَهْر shahr *(month)* نَهْر nahr *(river)*	أَشْهُر 'ashhur *(months)* أَنْهُر 'anhur *(rivers)*
CuCaCaa'	عَالِم xaalim *(religious scholar)* وَزِير waziir *(minister)*	عُلَمَاء xulamaa' *(religious scholars)* وُزَرَاء wuzaraa'*(ministers)*
'aCCiCaa'	صَدِيق Sadiiq *(friend)* قَرِيب qariib *(relative)*	أَصْدِقَاء 'aSdiqaa' *(friends)* أَقْرِبَاء 'aqribaa'*(relatives)*

D. THE DUAL FORM

Nouns also have a dual form, denoting two or a pair, which is regular in all cases and involves the ending ان -aan. Note that the "hidden t" of ة is pronounced before the dual ending.

وَلَد	walad	*boy (m. sg.)*
وَلَدان	waladaan	*two boys (m. du.)*
مُدَرِّس	mudarris	*teacher (m. sg.)*
مُدَرِّسان	mudarrisaan	*two teachers (m. du.)*
بِنْت	bint	*girl (f. sg.)*
بِنْتان	bintaan	*two girls (f. du.)*
مُدَرِّسَة	mudarrisa	*teacher (f. sg.)*
مُدَرِّستان	mudarrisataan	*two teachers (f. du.)*

2. PRONOUNS AND PERSONAL SUFFIXES

The personal pronouns in Arabic are:

أَنَا 'anaa *(I)*	نَحْنُ naHnu *(we)*
أَنْتَ 'anta *(you, m.)*	أَنْتُم 'antum *(you, pl, m. or mixed)*
أَنْتِ 'anti *(you, f.)*	أَنْتُنَّ 'antunna *(you, pl, f.)*
هُوَ huwa *(he)*	هُم hum *(they, m. or mixed)*
هِيَ hiya *(she)*	هُنَّ hunna *(they, f.)*
أَنْتُمَا 'antumaa *(you two, the two of you)*	هُمَا humaa *(those two, the two of them)*

There are also personal suffixes, which play a few roles. When attached to nouns, they are translated as possessive (*my book*). When attached to verbs or prepositions, they are translated as object pronouns (*see him*, *with him*). Here are all of the personal suffixes used with the prepositions عِنْدَ xinda, a construction that can be translated as *I have*, *you have*, etc.

عِنْدِي	xindii	*I have*
عِنْدَكَ	xindaka	*you (m.) have*
عِنْدَكِ	xindaki	*you (f.) have*
عِنْدَهُ	xindahu	*he, it has*
عِنْدَها	xindahaa	*she, it has*
عِنْدَكُمَا	xindakumaa	*you two have*
عِنْدَنَا	xindanaa	*we have*
عِنْدَكُمْ	xindakum	*you (m./mixed) have*
عندكُنَّ	xindakunna	*you (f.) have*
عِنْدَهُم	xindahum	*they (m./mixed) have*
عِنْدَهُنَّ	xindahunna	*they (f.) have*
عِنْدَهُمَا	xindahumaa	*the two of them have*

3. إضافة 'IDAAFA (POSSESSIVE NOUN PHRASES)

The construction "X of Y" or "Y's X" is translated in Arabic as إضافة 'iDaafa, also known as a possessive noun phrase or a construct. There are both indefinite and definite إضافة 'iDaafa. Indefinite إضافة 'iDaafa is formed by stringing two nouns together, first the thing possessed, and then the possessor.

بَيْت رَجُل	bayt rajul	*a man's house, a house of a man*
كِتاب بِنْت	kitaab bint	*a girl's book, a book of a girl*

Definite إضافة 'iDaafa is formed with the definite article preceding only the second noun, or the possessor. The definite article never appears before the first noun, even though it is interpreted as definite.

إسم الوَلَد	'ism al-walad	*the boy's name, the name of the boy*
بَيْت ألرَجُل	bayt ar-rajul	*the man's house, the house of the man*

Adjectives describing either member of the إضافة 'iDaafa must follow the entire construction. This may lead to ambiguity unless there is a gender or number mismatch between the possessor and the thing possessed.

بَيْت الرَجُل الكَبير	bayt ar-rajul al-kabiir	*the man's big house (using m. term for house) or the old/big man's house*
دار الرَجُل الكَبيرة	daar ar-rajul al-kabiira	*the man's big house (using f. term for house)*
دار الرَجُل الكَبير	daar ar-rajul al-kabiir	*the big/old man's house*

4. ADJECTIVES

A. POSITION AND AGREEMENT

Adjectives come after the noun they modify, and they agree in number, gender, and definiteness with that noun. Feminine singular adjectives add the ending ة -a. Adjectives agreeing with definite nouns take the definite article in exactly the same manner as do nouns.

صَديق لَطيف	Sadiiq laTiif	*a nice male friend*
الصّديق اللَّطيف	aS-Sadiiq al-laTiif	*the nice male friend*
صَديقَة لَطيفَة	Sadiiqa laTiifa	*a nice female friend*
الصّديقَة اللَّطيفَة	aS-Sadiiqa l-laTiifa	*the nice female friend*

In the plural, adjectives that have broken plural forms take the broken plural to modify masculine or mixed human plurals. Feminine human plurals take the sound plural ending ـات -aat. If an adjective does not have a broken plural form, for example many adjectives denoting nationalities, or adjectives that are longer than typical three-consonant Arabic roots, the sound plural ending ون -uun is used for masculines. Non-human plurals are modified by adjectives that take the feminine singular ending.

رِجال طِوال	rijaal Tiwaal	*tall men*
نِساء طَويلات	nisaa' Tawiilaat	*tall women*
رِجال مِصرِيون	rijaal miSriyuun	*Egyptian men*

كُتُب جَيِّدة	kutub jayyida	*good books*

B. IRREGULAR ADJECTIVES

Many common adjectives denoting colors have irregular feminine forms. In the following list, the masculine is given first, followed by the feminine.

أَبْيَض / بَيْضاء	'abyaD / bayDaa'	*white (m./f.)*
أَسْوَد / سَوْداء	'aswad / sawdaa'	*black (m./f.)*
أَخْضَر / خَضْراء	'akhDar / khaDraa'	*green (m./f.)*
أَزْرَق / زَرْقاء	'azraq / zarqaa'	*blue (m./f.)*
أَحْمَر / حَمْراء	'aHmar / Hamraa'	*red (m./f.)*
أَصْفَر / صَفْراء	'aSfar / Safraa'	*yellow (m./f.)*

C. DEGREES OF ADJECTIVES

The comparative and superlative share one form in Arabic, aCCaC, which remains the same regardless of the gender, definiteness, or number of the noun it modifies. The comparative lacks definite agreement.

ADJECTIVE	COMPARATIVE
كَبير kabiir *(big)*	أكبَر 'akbar *(bigger)*
ماهِر maahir *(clever, skillful)*	أمهَر 'amhar *(more clever, more skillful)*

أُحِبُّ هذا أفضَل.	'uHibbu haaDhaa 'afDal.	*I like this better.*
الرياضة أَفضَل مِن النُزهة.	ar-riyaaDa 'afDal min an-nuzha.	*Sports are better than walking.*

The superlative adds the definite article الـ al.

الأفْضَل	al-'afDal	*the best*
الأسوَأ	al-'aswa'	*the worst*
الأمْهَر	al-'amhar	*the most clever, the most skillful*

5. DEMONSTRATIVES

The forms of the demonstratives in Arabic are:

هَذا	haadhaa	*this (m.)*
هَذِه	haadhihi	*this (f.)*
هَؤلاء	haa'ulaa'	*these (pl.)*
ذَلِكَ	dhaalika	*that (m.)*
تِلْكَ	tilka	*that (f.)*
أُولَئِكَ	'ulaa'ika	*those (pl.)*

The plural forms هَؤلاء **haa'ulaa'** and أُولَئِكَ **'ulaa'ika** are used for both masculine and feminine people. Non-human plurals use the feminine singular forms هَذِه **haadhihi** or تِلْكَ **tilka**. Demonstratives can be translated as adjectives (*this book*) when linked with a noun by the definite article.

هَذا الكِتاب كَبير.	**haadhaa l-kitaab kabiir.**	*This book is big.*
هؤلاء الرِجال طِوال.	**haa'ulaa'i l-rijaal Tiwaal.**	*These men are tall.*

Or they can be translated as a pronoun (*this is a book*) when used with an indefinite noun.

هَؤلاء رِجال طِوال.	**haa'ulaa'i rijaal Tiwaal.**	*These are tall men.*
هؤلاء نِساء طَويلات.	**haa'ulaa'i nisaa' Tawiilaat.**	*These are tall women.*

6. NUMBERS

A. CARDINAL NUMBERS

صِفر	**Sifr**	*zero*
واحِد	**waaHid**	*one*
إثْنان	**'ithnaan**	*two*
ثَلاثة	**thalaatha**	*three*
أَرْبَعة	**'arbaxa**	*four*

خَمْسة	khamsa	*five*
سِتَّة	sitta	*six*
سَبْعَة	sabxa	*seven*
ثَمانِية	thamaaniya	*eight*
تِسْعَة	tisxa	*nine*
عَشَرَة	xashara	*ten*
أَحَدَ عَشَر	'aHada xashar	*eleven*
إثنا عَشَر	'ithnaa xashar	*twelve*
ثَلاثَة عَشَر	thalaathata xashar	*thirteen*
أَرْبَعة عَشَر	'arbaxata xashar	*fourteen*
خَمْسةَ عَشَر	khamsata xashar	*fifteen*
سِتّة عَشَر	sittata xashar	*sixteen*
سَبْعة عَشَر	sabxata xashar	*seventeen*
ثَمانية عَشَر	thamaaniyata xashar	*eighteen*
تِسْعة عَشَر	tisxata xashar	*nineteen*
عِشرون	xishruun	*twenty*
ثلاثون	thalaathuun	*thirty*
أرْبعون	'arbaxuun	*forty*
خَمسون	khamsuun	*fifty*
سِتّون	sittuun	*sixty*
سَبْعون	sabxuun	*seventy*

ثَمانون	thamaanuun	*eighty*
تِسعون	tisxuun	*ninety*
مِئة	mi'a	*one hundred*
أَلْف	'alf	*one thousand*
مِليون	milyuun	*one million*

B. ORDINAL NUMBERS

أوَّل، أولى	'awwal, 'uulaa	*first (m., f.)*
ثاني، ثانية	thaanii, thaaniya	*second (m., f.)*
ثالِث، ثالِثة	thaalith, thaalitha	*third (m., f.)*
رابِع، رابِعة	raabix, raabixa	*fourth (m., f.)*
خامِس، خامِسة	khaamis, khaamisa	*fifth (m., f.)*
سادِس، سادِسة	saadis, saadisa	*sixth (m., f.)*
سابِع، سابِعة	saabix, saabixa	*seventh (m., f.)*
ثامِن، ثامِنة	thaamin, thaamina	*eighth (m., f.)*
تاسِع، تاسِعة	taasix, taasixa	*ninth (m., f.)*
عاشِر، عاشِرة	xaashir, xaashira	*tenth (m., f.)*
حادي عَشَر، حادية عشرة	Haadii xaashar, Haadiyata xashra	*eleventh (m., f.)*
ثاني عَشَر، ثانية عَشْرة	thaanii xaashar, thaaniyata xashra	*twelfth (m., f.)*

7. QUESTION WORDS/INTERROGATIVES

مَا	maa	*what? (before a noun)*
مَاذَا	maadhaa	*what? (before a verb)*
أَيْن	'ayn(a)	*where?*
مِنْ أيْن	min 'ayn(a)	*from where?*
مَنْ	man	*who?*
مَتَى	mataa	*when?*
لِمَاذَا	limaadhaa	*why? (literally: for what?)*
كَيْفَ	kayf(a)	*how?*

8. COMMON PREPOSITIONS

مِنْ	min	*from*
فِي	fii	*in*
عِنْدَ	xinda	*at, also used to express have*
مَعَ	maxa	*with*
عَلَى	xalaa	*on*
إلَى	'ilaa	*to, toward*
قَرِيبْ مِنْ	qariib min	*near, close to*
تَحْتَ	taHta	*under*

بِجَانِبِ	bijaanibi	*next to*
وَرَاءَ	waraa'a	*behind*

9. VERBS

A. THE PRESENT TENSE

There are two main tenses in Arabic, the past and the present. The present tense is conjugated with both prefixes and suffixes, and a vowel between the second and third root consonant that must be memorized for each verb. Dictionaries will indicate this present tense vowel. There is no infinitive form in Arabic, so the third person singular of the past tense is usually used as the basic form of the verb in dictionaries, as it is the simplest form.

PRONOUN	PREFIX	SUFFIX
أنا 'anaa (*I*)	أَ 'a-	ُ -u
أَنْتَ 'anta (*you, m.*)	تَـ ta-	ُ -u
أَنْتِ 'anti (*you, f.*)	تَـ ta-	ينَ -iina
هوَ huwa (*he*)	يَـ ya-	ُ -u
هيَ hiya (*she*)	تَـ ta-	ُ -u
أنتُما 'antumaa (*the two of you, m. or f.*)	تَـ ta-	انِ -aani
نَحنُ naHnu (*we*)	نَـ na-	ُ -u
أَنْتُم 'antum (*you, pl.*)	تَـ ta-	ونَ -uuna
أَنْتُنَّ 'antunna (*you, f., pl.*)	تَـ ta-	نَ -na

هُم hum (*they, m.*)	يـَ ya-	ونَ -uuna
هُنَّ hunna (*they, f.*)	يـَ ya-	نَ -na
هُما humaa (*two of them, m.*)	يـَ ya-	انِ -aani
هُما humaa (*two of them, f.*)	تـَ ta-	انِ -aani

Here is the entire present tense conjugation of يَفْعَلُ yafxalu (*do/does*).

أَنَا أَفْعَلُ	'anaa 'afxalu	*I do*
أَنْتَ تَفْعَلُ	'anta tafxalu	*you (m.) do*
أَنْتِ تَفْعَلِينَ	'anti tafxaliina	*you (f.) do*
هُوَ يَفْعَلُ	huwa yafxalu	*he does*
هِيَ تَفْعَلُ	hiya tafxalu	*she does*
أَنْتُمَا تَفْعَلاَنِ	'antumaa tafxalaani	*you two do*
نَحْنُ نَفْعَلُ	naHnu nafxalu	*we do*
أَنْتُمْ تَفْعَلُونْ	'antum tafxaluuna	*you (m. pl.) do*
أَنْتُنَّ تَفْعَلْنَ	'antunna tafxalna	*you (f. pl.) do*
هُمْ يَفْعَلُونَ	hum yafxaluuna	*they (m.) do*
هُنَّ يَفْعَلْنَ	hunna yafxalna	*they (f.) do*
هُما يفعلانِ	humaa yafxalaani	*the two of them (m.) do*
هُمَا تَفْعَلاَنِ	humaa tafxalaani	*the two of them (f.) do*

B. THE PAST TENSE

The past tense is conjugated with a short -a- between the root consonants (and rarely an -i-) and a set of endings that change depending on the person. There is no prefix in the past tense.

PRONOUN	PREFIX	SUFFIX
أنا 'anaa *(I)*	—	ـتُ -tu
أنْتَ 'anta *(you, m.)*	—	ـتَ -ta
أَنْتِ 'anti *(you, f.)*	—	ـتِ -ti
هوَ huwa *(he)*	—	ـَ -a
هيَ hiya *(she)*	—	ـَت -at
أنتُما 'antumaa *(the two of you, m. or f.)*	—	ـتُمَا -tumaa
نَحنُ naHnu *(we)*	—	ـنا -naa
أَنْتُم 'antum *(you, pl.)*	—	ـتُمْ -tum
أَنْتُنَّ 'antunna *(you, f., pl.)*	—	ـتُنَّ -tunna
هُم hum *(they, m.)*	—	ـوا -uu
هُنَّ hunna *(they, f.)*	—	ـنَ -na
هُما humaa *(two of them, m.)*	—	ـا -aa
هُما humaa *(two of them, f.)*	—	ـَتا -ataa

Here is the entire past tense conjugation of يَفْعَلُ yafxalu (*do/does*).

أَنَا فَعَلْتُ	'anaa faxaltu	*I did*
أَنْتَ فَعَلْتَ	'anta faxalta	*you (m.) did*
أَنْتِ فَعَلْتِ	'anti faxalti	*you (f.) did*
هُوَ فَعَلَ	huwa faxala	*he did*
هِيَ فَعَلَتْ	hiya faxalat	*she did*
أَنْتُمَا فَعَلْتُمَا	'antumaa faxaltumaa	*the two of you did*
نَحْنُ فَعَلنا	naHnu faxalnaa	*we did*
أَنْتُمْ فَعَلْتُمْ	'antum faxaltum	*you (m. pl.) did*
أَنْتُنَّ فَعَلْتُنَّ	'antunna faxaltunna	*you (f. pl.) did*
هُمْ فَعَلُوا	hum faxaluu	*they (m.) did*
هُنَّ فَعَلْنَ	hunna faxalna	*they (f.) did*
هُمَا فَعَلاَ	humaa faxalaa	*the two of them (m.) did*
هُمَا فَعَلَتَا	humaa faxalataa	*the two of them (f.) did*